BIG

LEAVE EFFECT

BIG
LEAVES FOR EXOTIC EFFECT

STEPHEN GRIFFITH

GUILD OF MASTER CRAFTSMAN PUBLICATIONS

For Sara, Laura and Ben

First published 2003 by
Guild of Master Craftsman Publications Ltd,
166 High Street, Lewes,
East Sussex, BN7 1XN

Text © Stephen Griffith 2003
© in the work GMC Publications Ltd
Photographs © Stephen Griffith (unless otherwise stated)

ISBN 1 86108 262 2

British Cataloguing in Publication Data
A catalogue record of this book is available from the British Library.

Publisher: Paul Richardson
Art Director: Ian Smith
Editor: Graham Clarke
Designer: Mind's Eye Design Ltd, Lewes
Illustrations: Carrie Hill and Chris Halls
Typeface: Goudy

Colour origination by Viscan Graphics Pte Ltd, Singapore

Printed and bound by Kyodo Printing, Singapore

Acknowledgements

My interest in growing plants for foliar effect has come about from experience gained whilst working abroad in more favourable climates, where the atmosphere and mood of a garden is subjugated by bold foliage plants. Through my work here in the UK I have been involved from the outset in putting together restoration plans and development ideas for the historic Abbotsbury Sub-tropical gardens, in Dorset. It is here, working as gardens curator, that I have been able to experiment with the cultivation of unusual plants from all over the world.

I would particularly like to thank the following:

- Ilchester Estates for granting me the opportunity to use the gardens to collate and photograph most of the plant data for this book.

- David Constantine and Christine Smithee of KobaKoba nursery for their valuable help, expertise, and in-depth plant knowledge, especially with the plant families Musaceae and Zingiberaceae. I'd like to thank them also for allowing me to take photographs of plants at the nursery for use in this book.

- Max Warwick of '360vr Tours', who so kindly gave his professional photographic expertise and time, to help take some of the high quality photographs used in this book.

- Ian Watt for the use of slides from his plant photo library, and similarly my editor at GMC Publications Ltd., Graham Clarke, for use of two of his photographs.

- Mark Brent, head gardener at Lamorran House, St Mawes, for his tour of the garden and detailed information on some of the plants growing there.

- Similarly to Ian Wright, head gardener at Trenwaigton Gardens, Penzance, for allowing me access to photograph some of the choice plants within the walled garden.

- Dr John Kirby, for reading some of the original drafts and pointing me in the right direction.

- And finally, my thanks to the garden staff at Abbotsbury Sub-tropical gardens, who so diligently posed for some of the informative photographic sequences used in this book.

CONTENTS

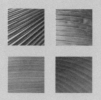

Introduction

This book is intended to be both a practical and visual guide for anyone interested in creating an exotic-looking garden in a cool, temperate climate. It focuses on all plants with large leaves, as well as plants that are considered to be architectural in form and shape. Both types help to create the backbone of the 'exotic'-looking garden. To generate this very stylized feel, we are attempting to mimic a jungle environment – big-leaved plants are often associated with the tropics.

This is not a book for the botanist, although occasional botanical references are used whilst giving descriptions. It is written for gardeners, landscape architects or nurserymen who, like me, have been seduced by the almost alien effect that can be achieved by integrating tropical-looking plants and large-leaved exotics into a landscape in a cooler climate.

The ability to travel to far-flung places has broadened our outlook, with so many new and glamorous locations opening up for tourism.

The perceived image of the tropics is of hot, steamy jungles with bromeliads growing along moss-laden branches high in the tree canopy. And of brightly coloured orchids, and huge swaying banana leaves dripping with moisture from the hot, humid and dank atmosphere. For many people it can evoke images of sun-kissed beaches and palm trees swaying in the breeze, with crimson-red hibiscus flowers in brown salt-glazed pots along the cool marbled foyer of an old colonial hotel.

The idea of trying to capture an image of this scene back home in our own gardens is very appealing. It may be more of a challenge to create, yet this garden style should be free of restrictions and conformity, allowing imagination and experimentation to develop.

1

Big-leaved plants

Gardening is an art loved by so many people from all walks of life, from the stately mansion owner, to the occupiers of more humble terraced houses, and even flat-dwellers who have to make do with a windowbox or two. Plants and gardens can appeal to people in different ways. For some, only the most colourful and brightest flowers merit their attention, for others it is the sheer pleasure of the herbaceous border, or of stately trees in an arboretum.

There are said to be over 26 million gardeners in the UK alone, all striving to grow plants that appeal to their own diverse tastes. This idiosyncratic approach to gardening has lead to the formation of so many new and specialized interest groups or societies, who are always on the lookout for new plants or improved cultivars. The search for knowledge, or inspirational ideas for planting and landscape design, can also be shared.

In recent years garden centres and shops have increased their range of plants with an ever-growing array of unusual imports from foreign nurseries. There were only a handful of sheltered mild gardens that grew tree ferns 20 years ago; nowadays you can't go anywhere without seeing them for sale, or sprouting out of highly decorative glazed containers on the balcony decking of some chic designer pub or restaurant.

We must, of course, thank the power of television, and the steady interest in garden makeover programmes, which has undoubtedly changed the image of gardening from the 'cloth cap and braces' era, to a younger generation that considers it 'the new rock and roll'. Following on from that, there is now a considerable amount of interest in, and an increasing passion for, growing a group of plants that is loosely termed 'the exotics'.

These are plants not to be confused with tender 'house plants' that originate from the tropics, although it is possible to use some of these outside in the warmer months.

The plants I'll be referring to throughout this book are exotic-looking species grown for their fine form and architectural foliage as much as for their flowers. Some may be half-hardy, and others totally frost-proof, but one common denominator is that they all add stature to the garden with their bold and dramatic leaves which have that sense of 'encounter' within the landscape.

There have been many books and catalogues produced looking at the more popular plants used by generations of gardeners. However, very few have been available specifically aiming at the 'exotic style', and even fewer if you narrow it down again to 'large-leaved exotics'.

In compiling this book I have used my working knowledge from managing Abbotsbury Sub-tropical gardens in Dorset, a mild garden on Britain's southern coast. It is here that I have had the opportunity to try out a wealth of plant material from all over the world, grown in a sheltered valley with its own very unique microclimate.

Some plants have flourished in the maritime climate, whilst others have perished from salt-laden winter gales. Heavy rains and waterlogged roots have been a bigger killer than the occasional cold spells of -6°C (21°F).

Only by throwing caution to the wind can we build up a working knowledge of which plants from warmer climates will succeed within our own given parameters of garden space or location.

The Chusan palm (Trachycarpus fortunei) — *adding that sense of 'encounter' in a woodland setting*

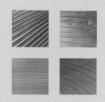

Form and structure

The sub-tropical garden can be established anywhere where the summers are warm and winters are mostly frost-free and mild. Generally, the plants associated with this type of garden have a strong visual impact and are actually the main architecture of the garden themselves. They are often evergreen, which gives a strong presence to the exotic-looking garden in winter.

LEFT: *An exotic planting scheme at the Lost Gardens of Heligan, Cornwall*
BELOW: *Sub-tropical bedding at the gardens of Hampton Court Palace, London*

Plants such as palms, bamboos and tree ferns all have good garden form and shape, which can take precedence over flowers. Their dimension and shape is also predictable, unlike shrubs. Plants such as bananas, with their huge leaves, are perfect for creating a bold statement in the landscape, where they are often used in sub-tropical bedding schemes.

It has long been understood that big leaves can broaden geometric and stylized patterns within planting schemes and make excellent accents to draw the eye as a focal point.

Large-leaved foliage forms

Some large-leaved plants can be made a feature in their own right. There are many hardy large-leaved plants that grow in cooler climates which can echo or mimic the bigger species from the tropical jungles. With careful selection it is possible to create a sub-tropical atmosphere by using plants not normally associated with this style of gardening, just as long as they have large leaves for adding drama. A balance can be struck by blending some of these into a planting scheme with other more traditional half-hardy exotics. This is also a good idea if you live in a particularly cold area, because it is vital to have some mainstay hardy plants that will keep the backbone of the garden alive should there be an exceptionally cold winter, with a high number of losses.

Mixing hardy foliage plants such as Hostas *with the more tender* Pseudopanax

Solid drifts of herbaceous groundcover will make a good foil with which to show off other more sculptural forms, and will also make good contrast when planted close to spiky leaved plants such as most types of *Yucca* and *Cordyline*. Of course, there are herbaceous plants, such as *Hosta* and *Farfugium*, with particularly good forms of leaf mottling, combined with splashes of lime green or golden variegation. These plants can be grown in dappled light conditions where, with careful positioning, the colour tones of the leaves will saturate light. They can even resemble the romantic shafts of sunlight that pierce through a jungle canopy.

A brief history of foliage plants

Gardening began as far back as 4000 years ago in Egypt and China. During the Han dynasty, the emperor Wu of China built vast lake and island gardens using natural rock features, symbolic of nature. In Egypt the fabulous gardens of Thebes and Luxor were tended by thousands of slaves. Over the centuries, decorating areas of land and growing plants for pleasure spread to other continents.

Ancient civilizations produced one of the seven wonders of the world with the Hanging Gardens of Babylon. Archaeological evidence has opened the historical debate on arguably the most amazing gardens the world had ever seen. They were created by Nebuchadnezzar for his home-sick wife Amytis in about 580BC. Her homeland was green and rugged, and she became depressed by the flat, sun-baked terrain of Mesopotamia. The King decided, therefore, to recreate her homeland by building an artificial mountain with vaulted terraces filled with earth. This magnificent rooftop garden became home to trees, luscious fruit and exotic foliage.

Now that's what I call creative landscaping, and it is the same principle we strive to achieve when setting out to create our own little sub-tropical paradise, reminding us of more exotic lands far away.

In the 15th century, trading ships brought back many exotic plants for wealthy Italian merchants in Venice and Genoa. Plants were being used to brighten up many of their grand houses. By the 16th century the Dutch, British, French and Germans took to the idea of growing exotic plants, but the plant that was really in fashion at the time was the orange.

This citrus plant was grown outdoors in large tubs for the summer, and overwintered in sheds heated by coal fires. Conditions were not perfect and many plants died. It was not until the 17th century that more elaborate buildings of stone and glass were purpose-built – the first orangeries. By the 18th century these structures had been refined into the first greenhouses, favourite places for the aristocracy, botanical gardens and keen horticulturists to grow their 'exotics'.

A 21st-century phenomenon that is the Eden Project, situated in Cornwall, in the far south-west of England. The domes are large enough to house an entire ecosystem. This is, to all intents and purposes, a modern orangery

This started a craze, and the race was on to find more unusual frost-sensitive exotics. Plant collectors roamed all over the world in search of new specimens. The interest in growing plants indoors started around 1820 when foliage plants like the fern, the palm and the aspidistra became popular. These plants were firm favourites with the Victorians.

Foliage plants were being chosen for their attractive leaves, and particularly where the leaves could retain a fresh look for long periods in an interior environment. This interest in exotic foliage plants eventually spread to the outdoor garden display, with plants such as bananas, yuccas, palms and many more glasshouse plants like coleus, philodendron, sansevieria, caladium and crotons, being planted outside for the summer.

This style of planting with a tamed jungle look can be described as 'sub-tropical bedding'.

A keen promoter of the 'wild garden' look in Victorian Britain was William Robinson. He wrote many gardening books, but in his 1871 book *The Sub-tropical Garden*, he described the use of exotics in the landscape. It was considered revolutionary at the time, but still holds fast today.

During the Victorian era, labour to tend these exotic collections was cheap. So, too, was the fuel to heat the glasshouses. This helped to continue the huge interest in foliage plants, especially as many new plants were being introduced from far-flung colonies. As a result, many new nurseries appeared specializing in the new ornamental exotic and foliage plants.

Some even had their own plant collectors, like the nursery of Veitch & Co of Exeter and London. This company employed two Cornish brothers, William and Thomas Lobb. In 1848 William travelled to South America where he brought back the Chilean fire bush (*Embothrium coccineum*), the Chilean lantern tree (*Crinodendron hookerianum*) and the monkey puzzle tree (*Araucaria araucana*), along with various flamboyantly coloured forms of *Begonia*. Thomas concentrated his search for plants in the Far East where he collected many exotic orchids and tender forms of *Rhododendron*.

In the United States the commercial exploitation of leaf plants can be traced back to 1880, when a limited number of growers began to use glasshouses to grow ferns and other foliage plants. In 1906 a Boston fern grower moved his business down to Florida when he recognized the potential for bulk growing in the mild climate.

All of this coincided with the advent of modernized homes with central heating, large picture windows, warm conservatories and the like, which have undoubtedly contributed to the growth of the foliage plant industry.

The cool sub-tropical climate

The English dictionary defines the term 'sub-tropical' as the region lying between the tropics and temperate lands. Temperate, meanwhile, is an area having a climate intermediate between tropical and polar; mild in quality or character, and exhibiting temperance. Although we don't all have the perfect climate to grow some of the more exotic and tender plants seen on our travels, as we will see in this book, it is possible to achieve the look and feel of the tropics in a cool, temperate garden.

The Mediterranean climate provides ideal conditions for growing sub-tropical plants. Here, the summers are hot and dry and often have drought, followed by winter rains. Plants from this region can become semi-dormant in summer and do all their growing in the winter. Parts of

the world that could be classed as having this high winter-rainfall Mediterranean-style climate include: California, South Africa, Southern Australia, coastal Chile, the Canaries, Madeira and, of course, all countries around the Mediterranean basin.

Sub-tropical plants also grow in areas where the rainfall occurs either mainly in summer, or perhaps all year round. In these places growth takes place in summer and dormancy in winter. These areas are found in South China, New Zealand, the Himalayan foothills, Florida and the Gulf Coast, the Pacific Islands, Mexico, South America and tropical Africa.

But what about the rest of us, who don't fit into either category?

Microclimates and other factors affecting the growing environment

The most important consideration when setting out to grow large-leaved exotic plants, especially the more tender species, is to have a thorough understanding of how your garden is affected in winter. This is particularly important if you happen to be gardening in a cooler area.

Inverewe Garden, in the north-western highlands of Scotland, is on the same latitude north (57.8°) as St. Petersburg in Russia and Hudson Bay in Canada, yet half-hardy plants flourish in the balmy microclimate

Gardens close to a large body of water, such as the sea or a freshwater lake, will have the advantage in that it will warm the adjacent land by one or two degrees in winter, enough to keep away some heavier frosts. The British Isles has a cool temperate maritime climate, and the western coast, in parts, is blessed with the warming effects of the North Atlantic drift, or Gulf Stream. This is a flow of water that originates from the Gulf of Mexico, and holds some of its warmth as it flows north-east across the Atlantic Ocean. That is why there are some remarkably mild gardens to be found in Ireland and even in the north-west highlands of Scotland, where palm trees can flourish along with many other tender plants from around the world.

The 'rain shadow' is another element associated with geographical location, and it can affect the development of a more exotic-looking garden. Clouds that form over the sea tend to condense into rain when they are blown over higher ground. The areas of land between the sea and the higher ground often have less rain and a higher than average number of sunshine hours. This provides a longer growing season during which the young growths of plants can ripen before the onset of winter, leaving them in a much better condition for the cooler times ahead.

If you have just taken on a new garden it is a good idea to have a few maximum/minimum thermometers placed around the plot in quite diverse locations. Surprisingly, the temperature, and therefore level of frost, can fluctuate wildly within a garden, meaning that some places are warmer than others. These warm spots are referred to as microclimates; areas that are generally warmer than the surrounding localities. They can range from a site only several metres in size, to a region within a country.

Buildings can significantly reduce the effects of frost on plants, as long as these plants are within 3m (10ft) or so of the walls. The sun's heat is stored in the stonework and this can warm the surroundings by radiation at night. This is why so many cities and suburban areas often have quite high mean temperatures in winter and surprisingly good microclimates. Heat produced by cars, central heating, lighting or any other similar source contributes to something called the heat island effect.

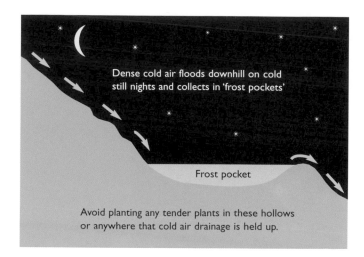

Dense cold air floods downhill on cold
still nights and collects in 'frost pockets'

Frost pocket

Avoid planting any tender plants in these hollows
or anywhere that cold air drainage is held up.

Winter blizzard on Phormium *and* Furcraea.
Many plants can recover from short periods of cold

Cold air is dense and runs downhill, so low-lying, open sites with no buildings, trees or high hedges are prone to frost settling in at night. This is called a frost pocket, and one of the worst sites will be at the bottom of a hill where the cold air collects. Avoid planting a hedge half-way down and parallel to the bottom ridge of a hill. This will trap cold air and form a frost pocket. Although buildings are beneficial generally, they may also contribute to the frost pocket effect if they are at the bottom of a hill.

Cold-hardiness in plants

The tolerance of plants to colder winter temperatures is influenced by many factors. It is difficult to be precise when predicting how hardy a plant is. There are many different types of conditions that might physically affect this, such as wet cold, dry cold, sudden cold or sustained wind chill. The age and size of the plant is important, too.

Some species have evolved with a degree of frost tolerance in their native habitats. This is usually found in high altitude plants. Low altitude species are adapted more to a warmer environment. The known provenance and the altitude at which the parent plant was collected are all key factors in determining the 'hardiness' of a plant.

In recent years our changing climate seems to be so unpredictable and, as so often happens, mild spells in the middle of winter trick many plants into early growth, which subsequently gets damaged by the next frost.

The position where a plant is growing will also determine how it copes with extreme winter cold. One school of thought is to avoid planting soft, fleshy plants where they might catch the early morning sun, as this early warmth will thaw out the plant's cells too quickly and hasten the breakdown and collapse of the whole plant.

Water

In many cases it is damp conditions rather than the cold that can induce rotting in a plant. By keeping some plants on the dry side, with good drainage in winter, their chance of survival is increased. This is especially true for succulent plants such as *Agave,* and fleshy-rooted and bulbous plants. Damp conditions, especially after a short mild spell, can also be perfect for the growth of powdery mildew, a fungal disease that can disfigure many types of plant. Spraying fleshy plants with a systemic fungicide will control its spread and help reduce rotting of the leaves.

Paradoxically, water can also be beneficial. The winter rains of northern Europe help keep minimum temperatures up, and provide useful moisture for areas where dry winds desiccate the ground in which evergreen exotics, such as palms, often suffer.

Plant size

Many half-hardy plants, especially palms, tend to be tougher and more able to cope with extreme winter chill if they have grown to a large size before being planted out. Growing on choice plants to a specimen size in large containers before planting out in the garden can be achieved by keeping them in a greenhouse over winter for several seasons. To avoid winter dormancy you must keep minimum temperatures to 5°C (41°F) to help sustain the plant growth. Regular feeding in the main growing season with, preferably, an organic slow release fertilizer, such as blood and bone or bonemeal will help increase leaf crown extension and promote strong roots.

Planting density

In many planting schemes overcrowding can spoil the overall effect. With the sub-tropical garden it can add to the semi-wild nature of the design. More important is the fact that close planting creates another microclimate within the border, and the close proximity of the plants creates a buffer zone which limits intense cold penetrating through.

Shelter

The first consideration for most large-leaved foliage plants is to provide a sheltered garden. Large evergreen trees or hedges can provide this shelter by filtering the wind and reducing its speed. They also have a huge warming effect in the garden. At Abbotsbury Sub-tropical gardens on the coast of southern England, there are many huge evergreen oaks (*Quercus ilex*). These act like a giant blanket over the garden in winter. By retaining their leaves, they help trap warm air and stop radiation frost creeping into the garden; any tender plants growing nearby will have a good degree of protection.

The choice of shelter-belt trees and hedging plants will depend on locality, climate and size of garden. It is considered most important to plant out shelter trees as very young specimens. Young trees growing in the ground make rapid root growth and firm anchorage. If they have been pot-grown for several years, the root system takes a longer time to establish. Some fast-growing species, such as *Eucalyptus,* can quickly become top-heavy, and so are liable to being blown down in a storm. These are best pruned by cutting out 40% of their top-growth after their first year. This takes weight off the crown and allows the root system to strengthen up.

Wind direction

No turbulence

It has been shown experimentally that a permeability of about 50% is ideal to filter the wind and avoid turbulence that could damage plants.

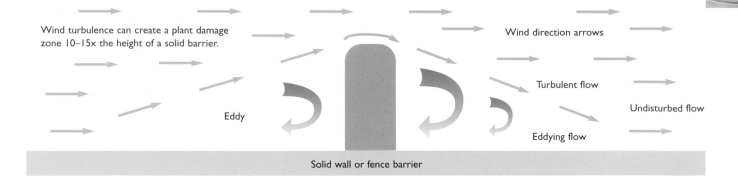

Wind turbulence can create a plant damage zone 10–15x the height of a solid barrier.

Wind direction arrows

Turbulent flow

Undisturbed flow

Eddy

Eddying flow

Solid wall or fence barrier

The provision of shelter also corrects other adverse effects of the wind – such as foliar scorching (especially maritime gardens with salt in the wind), water loss due to increased evaporation, heat loss and physical damage.

The above diagram shows the air-flow pattern produced by a solid wall barrier. An increase in wind turbulence can cause damage. An upward deflection of air occurs, resulting in air currents to the leeward side of the barrier. A more permeable barrier such as a hedge or tree shelter belt is desirable, therefore, and it has been shown experimentally that a permeability of about 50% is desirable.

This can be achieved by planting hedges or trees. However, perimeter fences made from woven polypropylene mesh, vertical wooden laths or coir netting, are just as good and can have some advantages. They do not compete with plants for nutrients and water from the soil, and they are effective immediately.

Winter preparations

At the end of summer when day length shortens and temperatures drop, tender or half-hardy plants will need some attention and preparation for the coming winter. The physiological state of a plant plays an important role with its ability to cope with the stresses of winter. Humans who endure low nutrition and poor housing will generally feel low and depressed. So, too, will a plant; it is more likely to succumb to cold and disease than a well-nourished 'happy' plant.

There are several very important rules:

- Avoid applying any fertilizer that is high in nitrogen just before the onset of winter. This promotes new growth that could get burned by an early frost.

- Increase the potash levels in both container plants and garden plants. Potash helps to harden the plants' cell walls to give better protection in low temperatures.

- Mulching around the base of any plant will help keep penetrating frost away from the roots. Mulches should be applied thickly enough to prevent light penetrating through, which will stimulate weed seeds into germination. Many materials can be used, such as gravels, water-worn pebbles, and organic by-products such as woodchips, bark, sawdust, rotted manure and seaweed. If woodchips are quite fresh then add some nitrogen-based fertilizer before applying. This counter-balances the loss of nutrients that the mulch uses as it rots down, which would otherwise be of detriment to the plants.

- Many different methods of wrapping plants up for winter can be used. Smaller plants that grow a metre high can have mini-tunnels

Mini-tunnels – used to protect tender plants in winter

A wigwam frame made from interwoven bracken or fern leaves. This makes good insulation against the cold, and the plant can 'breathe'

placed over them. These can be made from sections of stiff plastic water pipe, bent over and fixed to a wooden frame, then covered with polythene. It is important to allow for ventilation to control condensation. Too much dripping moisture can induce rotting and fungal attack. Ventilate by placing the whole mini-tunnel on bricks to give a minimum ground clearance of 10cm (4in). In really cold conditions the insides could be packed with dry straw for insulation.

- Where conditions are likely to become extremely cold, taller plants like tree ferns (*Dicksonia*) or bananas (*Musa*) can be individually wrapped. Breathable materials are preferred such as hessian, frost-protection fleece, old carpet or dried fern leaves. Plants like the New Zealand cabbage palm (*Cordyline australis*) can have their leaves tied up in a bundle to protect the crown. The giant leaves of *Gunnera manicata* can be folded together over the top of the crown as they die down, to help protect the main plant.

- For gardens in cold areas where the winters are unpredictable it is best to be on the safe side and 'lift' any plants that are on the borderline of hardiness. Or, take cuttings as an insurance against losses. Tuberous plants like *Hedychium*, *Canna* or *Dahlia* are best stored on the dry side in boxes of dry compost. Too much moisture might encourage the growth of the grey mould fungus. As a precaution against this infection you can dust the roots in sulphur powder before storage. As daylight lengthens towards the end of winter, a gentle watering will break their dormancy and new shoots will appear. The advantage of lifting and storing them overwinter is that the premature growth under glass will encourage earlier flowering over plants left in the ground for the coldest months.

Even large plants like this Ensete ventricosa *can be lifted and stored. Hessian sacking is used to hold the rootball together and help prevent the roots from drying out. Plastic dustbins are good for storing large rootballs*

Digging carefully around the rootball and lifting onto hessian sacking. This holds the soil together and protects the fine roots

Containerizing the plant in readiness for its storage over the winter

Pruning the tops off Canna *'Durban' before lifting and storing for the winter*

Bananas wrapped up for winter

Lifting tender sub-shrubs like Sparmannia africana for winter protection under glass

Cultural techniques

Sub-tropical bedding

If you are able to grow a selection of tropical house plants under glass, it is well worth considering planting some of them out in the garden for the warmer summer months. For example, fine foliage plants like *Cycad*, *Croton*, *Solenostemon* (coleus) and *Strelitzia*, or some of the elegant indoor feather palms, can all create that extra exotic look in the garden. Take care that they are not placed in bright direct sunshine for long periods of the day, which can scorch the leaves, or in a cold, windy part of the garden.

A good sack truck or one especially designed for large pots will help transport larger specimens

This technique of temporarily planting tender exotics out in the garden is referred to as 'plunge bedding'. Choice specimens can integrate into the established border with stunning effect, especially when worked with other compatible plants such as the Indian shot (*Canna*), the false castor oil plant (*Ricinus communis*) or *Arundo donax*.

As to precisely when you lift and repot these plants and take them back inside for the winter, this will depend very much on locality and climate.

Pruning for vigour

There are some trees and shrubs that can produce enormous tropical-looking leaves after being stimulated into growth by severe pruning in early spring. The best example is the Chinese foxglove tree (*Paulownia tomentosa*). This normally makes a handsome round-topped tree with heliotrope-like flowers. Alternatively, young plants can be severely pruned almost to the ground in spring. Many new shoots will form, but these should be thinned to one single shoot. This shoot can grow 2.5–3m (8–10ft) tall in one season and produce huge leaves up to 60cm (2ft) or more across.

This annual pruning is known as 'stooling'. Other species that can make a large leaf with an exotic look from this method are *Aralia elata*, *Ailanthus altissima* and *Catalpa bignonioides*. *Eucalyptus* will respond with lots of regrowth, however the new juvenile foliage is attractive but not necessarily larger leaved.

Paulownia *shoot after pruning*

Paulownia *showing two months' new growth*

Feeding plants

All plants need a good, balanced supply of food for the production of healthy leaves, roots and flowers. A good garden soil with plenty of organic matter will hold nutrients better than a depleted dry soil with no structure. So always add well-rotted organic matter, such as farmyard manure or garden compost, whenever possible.

Plant feed is mostly applied as a compound fertilizer, together with a well-balanced selection of plant feeding ingredients such as trace elements or organic extracts. They are made up of nitrogen (for healthy leaves), phosphates (for root development), and potash (for flower and, ultimately, fruit production). So, for bigger healthier leaves, look for a fertilizer that has a higher percentage of nitrogen in it.

Aesthetics and structure in the landscape

In order to create a broad image of the sub-tropics we must look at the cultural ethos and background of some of the plants we grow, and the importance of landscaping detail, which can enhance the garden and help promote the sub-tropical feel.

Garden buildings

These can set the scene, yet they need not be a major undertaking. With some careful thought, an ordinary garden shed could be transformed with a red-oxide roof and wooden veranda, the sort of wooden hut you might see in the Caribbean or in the outback of Australia. Even the most basic primitive beach shelters made of driftwood and thatched palm leaves could make an interesting scene set in amongst your palms, grasses and bananas. At least it will give your neighbours something to talk about!

Bamboo hut at the Bambouserie, France

The Old Colonial Tea House at Abbotsbury Sub-tropical gardens in Dorset, England. The setting makes it appear as though it really is in the tropics

Pots and containers

These have the advantage that they are mobile. The balance of the garden can be altered just by the simple presence of a well-placed pot and its contents. Containers can be moved around during the summer to enhance different corners of the garden, or if they are too heavy, then a more permanent site should be sought. Large pots in pairs compose a balanced feel and could be used at

the approach to garden steps, for example. Containers, with plenty of sharp grit for drainage, will make a good home for exotic-looking succulent plants, such as *Agave,* and in winter they can quickly be taken in under cover to give protection from severe weather.

There are many different types of kiln-dried terracotta pots. Some of the larger ones are handmade in Crete. Antique pithos and old olive oil 'beehive' pots from Greece, Portugal or Spain have a real mystery and attraction as relics of a bygone age. Vietnamese salt-glazed containers often come in darker rustic browns and black, usually with engraved patterns. Mexican pottery is attractive, tough and practical, and for something more adventurous, why not try a Mexican chiminea. This is an outdoor wood-burning fireplace that is ideal for the courtyard or patio.

Landscape materials

The 'hard landscaping', such as fencing, paths or stonework, has to have the right detail in order to enhance and pick up on the tropical theme. Bamboos are a good example. It is now possible to buy very attractive bamboo screening made either from split bamboo canes or whole canes, fixed together with stainless steel rustproof wire. They are relatively inexpensive, and can be used to revamp your existing fence panels.

For handrails on a terrace or bridge, bamboo poles can be the perfect answer. They add character to the garden as well as being a practical aid. They come in various diameters and colours that can range from black and blonde to a 'smoked' effect.

Agaves in pots. Don't forget to prune off the sharp needle-like tips if the plant is close to a pathway

Interior of the Eden Project: natural bamboo fencing is used for that authentic look

For an effective and stylish addition to planting schemes in courtyards, pool sides, or large containers, try using rounded pebbles as a mulch. They can be bought bagged, and in various sizes, from most builders' merchants. A more recent innovation is the use of worn slate pieces. The grey slate, that has been rounded by 'drum tumbling' for several hours in a cement mixer to leave masses of smooth-edged slate pieces, is ideal to spread under plants. It not only looks good but helps reduce moisture loss and weed growth.

Garden furniture

This should look like it has come straight out of the old colonial tropics. Stylish and comfortable

Rattan furniture comes from the south seas. Unlike bamboo, which is hollow, Rattan is solid, giving strength and durability. Polypropylene weaving is now available which can copy the 'Singapore'-styled chair, providing an attractive yet extremely durable, weather-resistant product. For an extra sense of decadence, an inviting hammock strung out under the shade of trees can really add a finishing touch.

Lighting

Night-time is often overlooked in the garden, except for the occasional barbecue. With subtle lighting, coloured filters and shadowy effects, large architectural evergreen foliage is at its best.

Uplighting from the ground projects a most effective light/shadow image. Lighting from above loses the ambience by throwing a white light over the subject, which can also blind the viewer. With careful positioning of lights, garden entertainment at night can take on a whole new meaning.

The Chusan palm (Trachycarpus fortunei)

Tree ferns and oak trees reflect mirror images onto the pond at Abbotsbury Gardens

Plant hardiness zones

When deciding if a particular plant is suitable for the climatic conditions of your garden, or even your part of the country, you will need to know two things. The first is the lowest range of winter temperatures that the plant can endure, and the second is the average coldest temperature for the area. Weather records and data have enabled horticulturists and botanists in America, from the Arnold Arboretum of Harvard University and the United States Department of Agriculture (USDA), to produce a detailed map based on temperatures for given regions, and the sorts of plants that will survive in them. A version of this map is printed overleaf. It is considered to be the standard measure of plant hardiness for most of the United States. There is also an equivalent zone map for Europe (see page 23), indicating the range of average annual minimum temperatures.

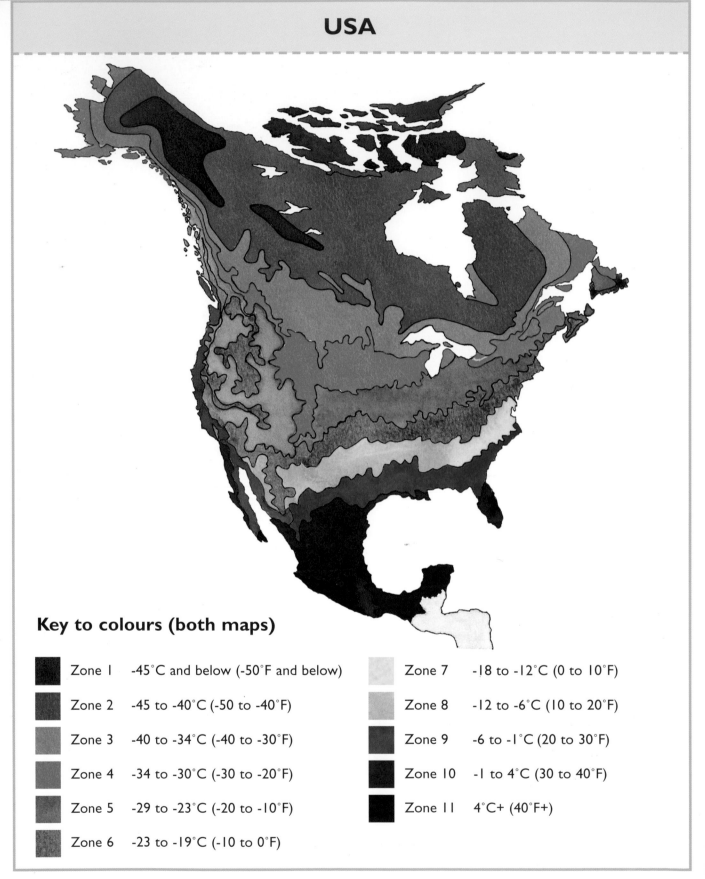

USA

Key to colours (both maps)

Zone 1	-45°C and below (-50°F and below)	
Zone 2	-45 to -40°C (-50 to -40°F)	
Zone 3	-40 to -34°C (-40 to -30°F)	
Zone 4	-34 to -30°C (-30 to -20°F)	
Zone 5	-29 to -23°C (-20 to -10°F)	
Zone 6	-23 to -19°C (-10 to 0°F)	
Zone 7	-18 to -12°C (0 to 10°F)	
Zone 8	-12 to -6°C (10 to 20°F)	
Zone 9	-6 to -1°C (20 to 30°F)	
Zone 10	-1 to 4°C (30 to 40°F)	
Zone 11	4°C+ (40°F+)	

Typical plant hardiness zones for North America

EUROPE

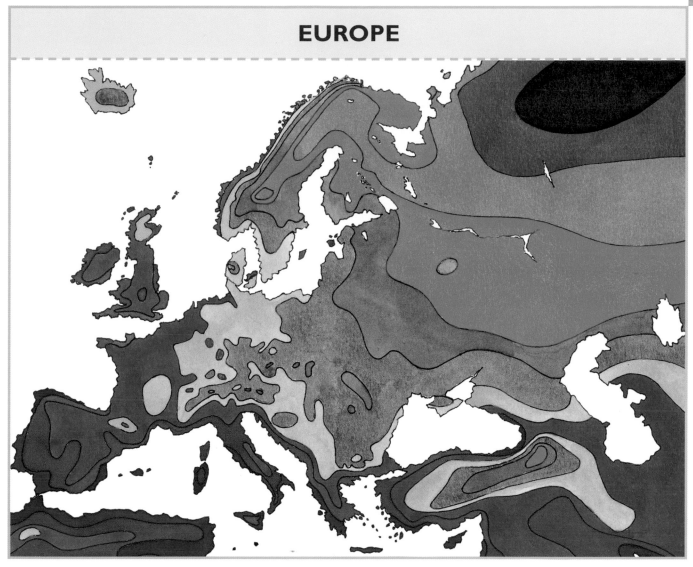

Typical plant hardiness zones for Europe

Climate change

There is an increasing awareness that global warming will have a real effect on climate change, with the possibility of a range of impacts on plant growth. Climatic records in the UK go back as far as 1659, and data shows an overall increase in temperature for the first 150 years after this date of 0.7°C.

In the 20th century, however, there is a jump of 10°C. This is due to human activity such as increased use of fossil fuels leading to higher concentrations of carbon dioxide and methane in the atmosphere ('greenhouse gases'). These gases block the planet's radiant energy from escaping, just like the glass roof of a greenhouse.

The effect for some of us will mean that there will be fewer frosts and higher mean temperatures, giving us greater scope to grow a wider range of 'sub-tropical' plants. Plants will also have to adapt to dryer summers and increased winter rainfall, therefore improved soil drainage will be a vital factor for many gardens in the future.

A-Z of large-leaved plants

This section of the book comprises a selection of photographs and descriptions of large-leaved plants, to help you make the right choices when creating your own exotic-looking garden. All commonly grown plant types are covered, from herbaceous perennials and trees and shrubs, through to the truly impressive palms, ferns, grasses, bamboos and succulents. The plants included in this section certainly do not rely solely on their leaves for effect. In fact, many have the added bonus of flowers that complement the large and interesting leaf forms.

A certain amount of experimentation may be needed to find out which plants may be suitable for one's own garden site. Obviously no two gardens are the same, especially when it comes to the climate. If you were to include some tropical house plants that could be 'plunged' outside during the summer months, you would add a great deal to the exotic effect.

This guide aims to focus on species that have had a track record of showing some tolerance to an average British summer and winter. Some plants featured here are totally hardy, yet they can contribute to the overall design and scheme of an exotic, temperate garden.

I have also included others that may well be worth a try, given the usual parameters of winter protection. Yet there is a strong element of the unknown. This style of gardening is all about experimenting with bold leaf forms, architectural shapes and audacious flower power.

To quote the well-worn proverb: beauty is in the eye of the beholder, and it applies to this subject as much as to any human connection. Individual tastes may differ, yet there is an overriding theme in that the tropical style is one of wild abandon where foreign exotics rub shoulders with more conventional garden plants to create luscious vegetation interspersed with alien plant forms.

Specializing and focusing on large leaves emphasizes their importance in the world of tropical garden style and highlights the character and change of ambience they can give to the garden. One other point to mention at this stage is the availability of the plants

discussed in this book. The vast majority will be readily available from garden centres or mail order specialist suppliers (a selection of the latter are listed on page 180).

There are some plants, however, which you may have a little difficulty in finding. Surely this is the very essence of what makes a plant so unique and special; where searching and sourcing is down to an individual's enthusiasm and persistence. Finding plants for the sub-tropical effect is not going to be a simple matter of popping down to the nearest garden centre or DIY superstore. Yet maybe through increased interest in the subject, and the popularity of books such as this one, this will be something to look forward to in the future.

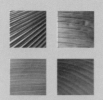

Herbaceous perennials A-Z

No garden can exist without a selection of herbaceous perennials – or 'border plants' if you prefer. Most are relatively low growing, but a few throw out dramatic flower spikes metres high. Some are choice, unusual and difficult to find plants; others are relatively common, and some even spread like weeds. But they all have one thing in common: impressive foliage.

Acanthus mollis

Family: Acanthaceae
Common name: Bear's breeches
Country of origin: Greece, Turkey and North-West Africa
Requirement: Position in full sun, although tolerant of shade
USDA Zone: Z6

A hardy perennial found growing in the wild on hot dry hillsides and banks, although it is quite tolerant of shade in the garden situation.

Acanthus produces stout clumps of glossy dark green leaves, which can be deeply cut or toothed and up to 25cm (10in) wide. They can make excellent ground cover colonies. The tall, prickly, purple and white flowers are very attractive, but you must remove the dead flower heads early in order to control self-seeding.

Botrytis or grey mould disease can occur over the leaves in damp summers, particularly if the site has little air movement. By pruning excess leaves away from neighbouring plants you will create a better air circulation which may reduce occurrence of the disease.

Acanthus mollis 'Hollard's Gold' is a good golden form, and is best grown in half-shade.

Acanthus mollis *'Hollard's Gold'*

Acanthus mollis

Amicia zygomeris

Family: Leguminosae – Papilionaceae
Common name: None
Country of origin: Mexico
Requirement: A position in full sun
USDA Zone: Z8

This attractive shrubby perennial is not exactly a large-leaved exotic but it has been included in this selection because of its unique foliage. It has pinnate, compound leaflets each 6cm (2¹/₂in) long and with a cleft tip. The stems produce leaf-like bracts, which are yellow-splashed and suffused with purple (an unusual combination), followed by pea-like yellow flowers in late summer. The whole plant will often die down to the ground after light frost but will regenerate in the spring. *Amicia* is tolerant of drought conditions and likes well-drained soil in a warm sunny site. Protect the roots in winter with a thick mulch of woodchip or bracken.

Amicia zygomeris

Aspidistra elatior

Family: Liliaceae
Common name: Cast-iron plant
Country of origin: Himalayas to Japan
Requirement: A shady place out of full sun
USDA Zone: Z7

In Victorian days *Aspidistra* was a very popular house plant. It is still recognized by everyone as that indestructible and often neglected foliage plant seen hiding in the corner of a dark hallway. It makes an excellent specimen for the cool glasshouse, conservatory or the home, yet is seldom tried outdoors.

The leaves are large, narrow and glossy. As a single specimen, *A. elatior* 'Variegata' makes a striking specimen. In the garden where winter temperatures rarely fall below -5°C (23°F) aspidistras can make wonderful bold-leaved ground cover. They are best planted in shade and at the base of a wall for shelter. They benefit from additional leafmould and a dilute liquid fertilizer in the growing season, and need a well-drained soil.

They do suffer from slug and snail damage when grown outside, and strangely enough it is said that these molluscs pollinate the rather drab aspidistra flowers.

Propagate by division in the spring.

Aspidistra elatior *'Variegata'*

Aspidistra elatior *'Milky Way'*

Astelia chathamica

Family: Liliaceae – Asteliaceae
Common name: None
Country of origin: Chatham Islands, New Zealand
Requirement: Moisture-retentive soil
USDA Zone: Z9

Often seen as *Astelia chathamica* 'Silver Spear', this is a superb perennial with handsome rosettes of silvery swordlike, arching leaves 50–200cm (20–78in) long and 5–10cm (2–4in) across. The flowers are really quite insignificant, being outshone by their orange fruits some 1cm (¹/₂in) in diameter.

This is a great plant to use as a foil, with its stunning silver foliage often used as background to other plants.

It can grow in sun or semi-shade, but it does require a good moisture-retentive soil. In its native habitat it grows in wet, peaty soil. It can be propagated by division in spring.

Astelia grandis is another very large-leaved species that requires similar conditions.

Astelia chathamica

Astelia grandis

Begonia grandis subsp evansiana

Family: Begoniaceae
Common name: Hardy begonia
Country of origin: Malaysia, China, Japan
Requirement: A position in partial or full shade
USDA Zone: Z6

This plant is perfect for that shady spot, perhaps in a woodland garden under trees. It has copper-green, ovate leaves up to 15cm (6in) long, erect stems up to 1m (3ft) in length, and pendant scented flowers in pink or white. It has the same appearance as its house plant cousins, yet can survive -5°C (23°F) in its dormant state. The whole plant dies down at the end of the season leaving small bulbils formed on the stems. These can be potted up for the following year, although the tuberous roots can be divided.

Begonia grandis *subsp* evansiana

Bergenia ciliata

Family: Saxifragaceae
Common name: None
Country of origin: Afghanistan to Kashmir
Requirement: A position in full sun or partial shade. Tolerant of high winds
USDA Zone: Z7

The familiar *Bergenia* is not a plant that says 'tropical' immediately, but it does makes a more hardy alternative for evergreen ground cover (although early flowers and young leaves can get frosted). In the wild this plant is found growing in damp, rocky woodland. The basal leaves are rounded, bristly, and up to 32cm (13in) across. Flowers are pale pink often deepening with age. It will grow in sun or part shade and prefers a moist soil, although it does seem to tolerate dry soils – and neglect – quite well.

Bergenia ciliata

Cynara cardunculus

Family: Compositae
Common name: Cardoon
Country of origin: South-West Europe, North Africa
Requirement: A position in full sun
USDA Zone: Z8

These plants make large, imposing, architectural clumps in the garden, with handsome, deeply dissected, grey leathery leaves growing up to 1m (3ft) long. Native to the Mediterranean and Morocco, they prefer full sun in a light, well-drained soil. Although hardy, they benefit from a mulch of well-rotted manure before the weather drops too low, to protect the roots. Keep the plants well watered in the summer.

They produce giant thistle-like, spiny purple-tinged florets. However, to grow large attractive leaves successfully for the foliage effect, it is best to remove the flowering stems. This also seems to help prevent the plant opening up too much and flopping in the height of summer.

Added benefits are that the young leaves can be blanched and eaten boiled. Of course its better known cousin is the globe artichoke (*Cynara cardunculus* Scolymus Group), which makes a bold tropical-looking specimen in a mixed border. The vegetable qualities of this plant need no introduction.

With both species, the silvery grey of the foliage is a great foil for plants of other colours, particularly blues, mauves and pinks. The cultivar 'Glauca' is particularly good.

Cynara cardunculus

Echium pininana

Family: Boraginaceae
Common name: Pride of the Canary Isles
Country of origin: Canary Islands
Requirement: A position in full sun or part shade; needs protecting from frost
USDA Zone: Z9

A plant of immense stature and presence in the garden, with its coarse, hairy, elongated basal leaves, which can get to 12cm (4¹/₂in) in width and 45cm (18in) in length. The giant bold flower spikes of blue to mauve are quite spectacular, towering up to around 4m (12ft) in ideal conditions.

There are over 40 species of *Echium*, from annual and biennial, to perennial herbs and sub-shrubs. In my experience *E. pininana* can behave as a biennial, perennial or even a sub-shrub in cooler climates, depending on the preceding winter or planting location.

Given a coastal location or a sheltered microclimate, I have seen them survive frosts of -4°C (25°F) where the leaves have all drooped. Provided the period of cold is not a long one, they recover quite quickly and will even self-seed around the garden. It is a native of La Palma, Canary Islands, where it grows amongst the laurel forests. This is a good indicator that they can be planted under trees for added winter protection, especially evergreen trees like the holly oak (*Quercus ilex*), the leaves of which act as a warming blanket in winter. Of course, *Echium* still enjoys a hot sunny spot in the garden.

Echium pininana *flower heads*

Early season foliage of Echium pininana

Eomecon chionantha

Family: Papaveraceae
Common name: Snow poppy
Country of origin: Eastern China
Requirement: A position in part shade
USDA Zone: Z7

This is a great plant for colonizing the woodland floor, under established trees and shrubs, or in shady borders. The glaucous foliage, with attractive wavy edges, is quite fragile and almost succulent. When snapped it will ooze an unusual orange sap. The individual leaves grow up to 10cm (4in) – not that big, but when grown en masse they have that jungle floor look.

The poppy flowers are white, and produced on nodding stems in spring. Where space permits it is great for ground cover, but it does have spreading rhizomes which might become a little invasive if it likes the conditions.

It does like sufficient moisture to establish, yet good drainage helps it in the winter. Cool, moist fertile soils with plenty of natural leaf mould and a shady position are the main requirements. Propagate by division in spring.

Eomecon chionantha

35

Eryngium

Family: Umbelliferae
Common name: Agave eringoe
Country of origin: United States, South America, Europe
Requirement: A position in full sun
USDA Zone: Z7

There are 230 species of *Eryngium*, found growing in a variety of habitats and nearly all requiring perfect drainage. *Eryngium agavifolium* has spiny toothed leaves which resemble *Agave* (hence the species name), and which are up to 75cm (30in) long. The green-blue, thistle-like flowers are rounded, and held on 70cm (28in) long stems. In its natural habitat it is found growing on stony hills and dry river banks. It is hardy to -10°C (14°F) but resents wet, poorly drained soil which can cause the plant to rot, especially after a wet winter.

Eryngium pandanifolium var *lasseauxii*, has weakly spined, basal leaves up to 1.5m (5ft) in length. It is a very architectural plant, with tall flower stems producing rounded, whitish flowers 1cm ($^{1}/_{2}$in) across. Native to southern Brazil and Uruguay, it is found growing in damp, grassy fields. This species is not quite so fussy about good drainage, although this does help it to survive low temperatures.

Eryngium agavifolium

Eryngium pandanifolium *var* lasseauxii

Farfugium japonicum

Family: Compositae
Common name: Leopard plant
Country of origin: Eastern Asia, Japan
Requirement: A partly shaded position in moisture-retentive soil; frost protection in winter
USDA Zone: Z9

Farfugium is a very useful evergreen perennial herb, occurring in the wild along streamside meadows and even growing quite close to the sea in Japan. It grows in dense colonies but is not as invasive as it looks. The leaves can grow to 5–30cm (2–12in) in width.

Farfugium japonicum 'Aureomaculatum' has remarkable white or yellow blotches on the leaves, as if bleach has been splattered over them. The form 'Argenteum' has a dark green centre surrounded by irregular silvery white variegation, and 'Crispatum' has crinkled edges to the leaves, rather like a fancy salad lettuce. All three make an exellent addition to the sub-tropical style ground cover, and can survive winter temperatures as low as -6°C (21°F), or even colder with a protective mulch of organic matter. *Farfugium* is best grown in a cool, moist, shady site as its leaves can collapse under hot, dry conditions. Most also make good pot plants if kept well watered.

Farfugium japonicum *'Aureomaculatum'*

Farfugium japonicum *'Argenteum'*

Farfugium japonicum *'Crispatum'*

Heracleum mantegazzianum

Family: Umbelliferae
Common name: Giant hogweed
Country of origin: South West Asia
Requirement: A moisture-retentive soil
USDA Zone: Z6
Caution: Can cause skin blistering on some people, and has been known to become a widespread and dangerous weed

Anyone with an eye for statuesque plants with great architectural qualities cannot fail to be impressed by this giant of a perennial plant. Suited to waterside plantings, large shrubberies or wild jungle-like areas, it has tall flowering stems up to 3.5m (11ft) high. Massive white umbels form the flowers that show in early to mid-summer, together with large pinnately lobed leaves to 1.3m (4^1/$_2$ft) across.

This is not a plant for the timid, however. It has a fearsome reputation for causing blistering when skin comes into contact with the leaves. Also, it has become a widespread and dangerous weed; as an escapee from gardens in the UK it has been found rapidly spreading in waste places and near streams. In both of these cases, sensible precautions should be taken.

Spreading seedlings can easily be controlled by hoeing or spot treatment with a translocated broadleaf herbicide. If you keep the plant to the back of the border, away from paths, where it can form a great backdrop for smaller plants in front of it, you are less likely to brush against it by accident. When you need to handle it use gloves to avoid contact with any of the sap, which can react on the skin and cause meadow dermatitis, especially in bright sunlight and warm temperatures. Avoid growing it where children are around.

Heracleum mantegazzianum

Hosta (cultivars)

Family: Hostaceae
Common name: Plantain lily
Country of origin: Japan, China, Korea
Requirement: A partly shaded position in moisture-retentive soil
USDA Zone: Z5

There are 40 species of *Hosta* and over 1,000 cultivars in all forms and combination of leaf size and colour. Some forms have round, heavily puckered foliage, which makes sumptuous clump-forming mounds. They even have quite attractive flowers.

For the woodland garden or more exotic themes, these large and luscious foliage plants are well suited, especially when growing in a cool, temperate climate.

Hosta 'Sum and Substance' has enormous smooth lime-green to pale yellow leaves. *Hosta sieboldiana* var *elegans* has rounded, bluish leaves which are deeply puckered and measure 30cm (12in) wide by 35cm (14in) long, and *Hosta* 'Big Daddy' has rounded, glaucous-blue leaves up to 45cm (18in) in length.

They are shade-loving plants and suit the dappled light of woodland conditions for growing luxuriant foliage. However, if planted in the sun they tend to produce more flowers.

Hosta thrives in a fertile soil, especially when enriched with well-rotted manure, and a ready supply of moisture which encourages good growth. The only drawback with these robust herbaceous perennials is that they are readily devoured by slugs, snails, deer and rabbits. Good plant hygiene and regular applications of proprietary slug-killing pellets around the plants keeps some order.

Hosta *'Sum and Substance'*

Impatiens tinctoria

Family: Balsaminaceae
Common name: Balsam
Country of origin: Uganda, Kenya, Ethiopia
Requirement: A partly shaded position in moisture-retentive soil; frost protection is required
USDA Zone: Z9

This is a relative of the more common free-flowering busy lizzie, but this species grows as a tuberous perennial with tall fleshy stems 1–2m (3–6ft) tall. The flowers are large and white with a red-pink blotching at the base. This is not a particularly big-leaved plant, but it has a fairly impressive overall structure, with oval to lanceolate leaves up to 18cm (7^1/$_2$in) long. Grow it on a moist soil in a partly shaded site with some shelter from the worst of the weather. Easily propagated from summer cuttings. Keep the root system thickly mulched to protect from winter frost.

Impatiens tinctoria

Inula magnifica

Family: Compositae
Common name: None
Country of origin: Caucasus
Requirement: A position in full sun or part shade; moisture-retentive soil
USDA Zone: Z6

A perennial, with yellow daisy flowers. Leaves are elliptic to ovate, up to 25cm (10in) wide. The plant forms a bold, solid clump that dies down in winter, leaving dead skeletal flower stalks. It will naturalize itself from seed. It also develops a vigorous, rhizomatous rootstock which could, in time, overtake nearby smaller perennials. *Inula helenium* is another large-leaved plant, commonly known as elecampine, and chiefly grown for its medicinal properties.

Inula magnifica

Kniphofia

Family: Liliaceae
Common name: Red hot poker
Country of origin: South Africa
Requirement: A position in full sun
USDA Zone: Z7

Red hot pokers have always been a favourite for the herbaceous border, with their bright, vibrant, fiery hot orange, red and yellow poker-shaped flowers. There are, however, two species that may be grown for their foliage only.

Kniphofia caulescens has glaucous-grey, strap-shaped leaves up to 60cm (2ft) long, produced on short, fleshy stems – almost leek-like in appearance and quite distinctive. The flowers are combined of two colours, peachy orange and cream-white. Native to the South African highlands at altitudes of up to 3,000m (1,083ft), these plants grow in colonies in peaty soil that overlies the rocky landscape.

The second poker to recommend is *Kniphofia northiae*, a robust, non-clump forming species, with broad, flat, evergreen leaves, growing in a rosette up to 1.5m (5ft) long and 5–10cm (2–4in) wide. The flowers start reddish pink in bud, opening creamy white to pale yellow, but in my experience they appear only very fleetingly. This species grows in wet peaty soil on grassy slopes and gullies in the mountainous regions of Natal, Lesotho and Cape Province.

Kniphofia northiae

Kniphofia caulescens

Ligularia

Family: Compositae
Common name: Leopard plant
Country of origin: China, Japan
Requirement: A position in part shade; requires a moisture-retentive soil
USDA Zone: Z5

Ligularia is a tough, hardy plant that can be grown both for its wonderful foliage and the yellow-orange, wand-like flowering stems. It is not often thought of as an exotic-looking species, but for the purpose of big leaves and jungle mimicry it is worth a try. There are 180 species of these perennial plants, many with large leaves, requiring a deep, moist and humus-rich soil.

Ligularia dentata has rounded, deeply cordate basal leaves to 30cm (12in) long and 38cm (15in) wide, on long stems, from a tufted rootstock. There are several named cultivars, such as 'Desdemona' with purple leaves, 'Dark Beauty' with very dark plum-green leaves, and 'Golden Queen' with green leaves and bright, golden flowers.

The garden form of *Ligularia* known as 'The Rocket' is a native of Japan, northern China and Taiwan. This plant has triangular leaves 24cm (9in) wide and 26cm (10in) long, with irregular serrated edges. It grows into large clumps that can be divided in the spring, and its flowers form as yellow trusses on 1.8m (6ft) long black stems.

When planted en masse they look good in a dappled woodland garden. If grown in more open sites they can wilt very quickly, especially on bright, windy days.

Ligularia dentata *'Desdemona'*

Ligularia stenocephala *'The Rocket'*

Lobelia tupa

Family: Campanulaceae
Common name : Lobelia
Country of origin: Chile
Requirement: A position in full sun; good plant for a coastal garden
USDA Zone: Z8

Lobelia tupa is an upright perennial developing tall terminal racemes with attractive broadly lanceolate leaves, covered in dense tomentum. Each leaf can be 30cm (12in) long. The tubular flower spikes are reddish scarlet and open from the base of the inflorescence upwards over a long period. In the wild these plants inhabit the coastal regions of Chile. They like full sun, a moisture-retentive soil, shelter and good drainage. The crowns will need some protection in winter, with bracken or woodchippings.

Lobelia tupa

Macleaya cordata

Family: Papaveraceae
Common name: Plume poppy
Country of origin: China, Japan
Requirement: A position in full sun
USDA Zone: Z3
Caution: Can be invasive

A tall, bold, attractive perennial with large foliage; ideal for the back of the border. The leaves are glaucous grey above, downy white beneath. They are rounded, with deeply lobed edges, 20cm (8in) across. The flowers are creamy white on plume-like panicles in summer. It is hardy, yet looks at home with the best of the semi-tropical plantings. It does, however, have a nasty habit of popping up all over the place, with its creeping rhizomes.

Macleaya cordata

Myosotidium hortensia

Family: Boraginaceae
Common name: Chatham Island Forget-me-not
Country of origin: New Zealand, Chatham Islands
Requirement: A partly shaded position; good for coastal gardens
USDA Zone: Z8

This is a plant that is endemic to the sandy and rocky coastline of the Chatham Islands, just east of New Zealand. It is grown for its shiny, deeply veined foliage, and its large dense heads of blue or white flowers reminiscent of forget-me-nots.

The leaves can get 20–40cm (8–16in) across with sprawling, flowering stems to 60cm (2ft) in length, and the flowers up to 2cm (³/₄in) across.

It is best grown where it can be kept cool, preferable semi-shaded in mid-summer. In winter it will need some protection if temperatures fall below -5°C (23°F). A covering of dry bracken, woodchips or evergreen branches should suffice. The soil should be free draining with plenty of humus, manure or peat incorporated. *Myosotidium* benefits from being given a liquid feed during the growing season and, if available, a good mulching of rotted seaweed. A little sea-sand applied around the crown of the plant is also beneficial.

Myosotidium hortensia

Petasites japonicus var giganteus

Family: Compositae – Asteraceae
Common name: Butterbur
Country of origin: Korea, China, Japan (naturalized in Europe)
Requirement: A position in part shade; a moisture-retentive soil
USDA Zone: Z5
Caution: Can be invasive

There are over 15 species of this perennial herb. The name comes from *Petasos*, Greek for 'a broad-brimmed hat', a reference to the leaf shape. All have rampant, invasive rhizomes, but despite their dangerous root systems there are some with great garden appeal.

Petasites japonicus var *giganteus* is one of them. It was a favourite with Victorian gardeners, who adored it for its giant leaves which measure 1–1.5m (3–5ft) across on tall leaf stalks up to 2m (6ft) long. The rounded and somewhat downy leaves can look very impressive when grown en masse, but it is really suited to the moist and shady parts of the wild woodland garden, or at the waterside where it will grow into stately colonies.

It is not a plant for small gardens and is, arguably, best grown in large containers with a sufficient size for a good root run, or in a raised bed where it can't escape.

Avoid planting these plants in direct sunlight as their large leaves will flop in the heat. *Petasites* likes any deep, fertile, moist soil, ideally with plenty of leaf mould or other humus to prevent the ground drying out.

Petasites japonicus *var* giganteus

Petasites japonicus *var* giganteus *'Nishiki-buki'*

Rheum palmatum

Family: Polygonaceae
Common name: A relative of the common culinary rhubarb (*Rheum* x *cultorum*)
Country of origin: China
Requirement: A position in full sun or part shade; a moisture-retentive soil
USDA Zone: Z6

The leaves are large and deeply cut. These are followed by tall deep red flower spikes which, if allowed to retain their seed heads, give an extra attraction later in the year. They can make impressive focal plants, especially as waterside plantings – they prefer a moisture-retentive soil containing plenty of humus.

The cultivar 'Atrosanguineum' has leaves that are a vivid red from the time they emerge in the spring; this colour is retained on the underside of the leaves until flowering time.

Rheum palmatum

Salvia hierosolymitana

Family: Labiatae
Common name: None
Country of origin: Lebanon
Requirement: A position in full sun
USDA Zone: Z8

Salvias are shrubby and herbaceous perennials with long-lasting ornamental flowers. Some, including this one, produce quite large and attractive foliage that is often overlooked. The large, hairy, oval, dark green leaves 25cm (10in) long, grow in clumps, and are followed by beautiful lavender-blue flowers on tall erect stems up to 1m (3ft) in height. It requires a warm, sheltered site with a light, free-draining soil. It can stand light frost. Once established, it can self-seed freely around the garden.

Salvia hierosolymitana

Senecio petasitis

Family: Compositae
Common name: None
Country of origin: Mexico
Requirement: A position in full sun or part shade; needs frost protection in winter
USDA Zone: Z9

This is an attractive perennial with soft, downy leaves some 10–25cm (4–10in) long and wide, lobed on the margins and veined. It may be found under its old name of *Roldana petasites*. In the spring it produces multi-clustered yellow daisy flowers. Although it is a sun lover, it can grow quite happily under the canopy of trees and tall shrubs, which can be specially useful during winter, as some protection against the cold may be afforded by this cover. The minimum winter temperature should be no lower than -3°C (27°F).

Senecio petasitis

Symphytum 'Goldsmith'

Family: Boraginaceae
Common name: Comfrey
Country of origin: Garden hybrid
Requirement: A position in part shade; needs a moisture-retentive soil
USDA Zone: Z5

The most commonly grown forms of *Symphytum* have coarse, hairy leaves up to 45cm (18in) long and 15cm (6in) wide. There are, however, attractive creamy variegated forms, such as 'Goldsmith'. Its leaf edges are beautifully splashed with gold and cream. The flowers can be pale blue, white or pink, but these are best removed early to enable the plant to put more of its energy into production of the foliage. It can be most impressive. This is a perennial herb, suited to shady and damp habitats. Propagate by division in spring.

Symphytum *'Goldsmith'*

Trachystemon orientalis

Family: Boraginaceae
Common name: None
Country of origin: Eastern Europe
Requirement: A position in full sun or part shade
USDA Zone: Z6

This handsome plant is a good for ground cover, with immense, coarse, hairy heart-shaped leaves 25–30cm (10–12in) across. The flowers are blue and similar to borage, carried on hirsute stems in early spring, before the leaves emerge.

For anyone creating an exotic-style garden in a shady area, and desiring of large-leaved plants like those of the *Hosta*, yet are plagued with slugs and snails, then *Trachystemon* could make a good alternative. It is pest resistant, tolerant of dry shade or sun, and will even endure either moist or dry soil.

The leaves are, however, prone to some wind scorch and they can become slowly invasive with a creeping root system and an ability to self-seed, but they are easy enough to control. This plant is especially good for the larger landscape where it can, when planted in groups, make big drifts and combine well, providing a contrast for more architectural, spiky subjects.

Trachystemon orientalis

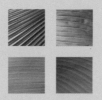

Small trees and shrubs A-Z

Shrubs and small garden trees can provide a permanent, living framework to a garden. Many shrubs used in a sub-tropical style garden will hold interest all year round with their luscious evergreen foliage and bold, impact-creating outlines. The selection in this chapter shows some of the more choice plants available. Some may be fairly common; some are rare. Others are slightly tender and only worth trying in colder locations provided winter protection is given.

Abutilon

Family: Malvaceae
Common name: Indian mallow, Flowering maple
Country of origin: Africa, Americas, Asia, Australia
Requirement: A position in full sun or part shade
USDA Zone: Z8

Although not the largest of foliage plants, *Abutilon* makes an excellent accompaniment within the mixed sub-tropical border. Known primarily for its attractive bell-shaped flowers, there are many cultivars with comparatively large leaves and interesting mottled vine-shaped leaves. *Abutilon* 'Cannington Peter' has spotted yellow and green leaves; *A. pictum* 'Thompsonii' has more yellow in its mottled leaves, as well as orange flowers. *Abutilon* 'Souvenir de Bonn' is a taller plant with bold, broadly white-margined foliage and orange bell flowers with dark veining.

They all like full sun to half-shade, preferably by a south-facing wall for shelter and warmth. Pruning the lateral shoots, which tend to be brittle and snap easily in high winds, will strengthen the crown. This pruning also promotes new growth, on which the flower buds are formed.

Aucuba japonica

Family: Cornaceae
Common name: Spotted laurel
Country of origin: China, southern Japan, Taiwan
Requirement: A partly shaded position; a good plant for coastal gardens
USDA Zone: Z7

A tough, indestructible, hardy, evergreen shrub well suited to dry shade or exposed sites.
Its large waxy leaves were very popular with the Victorians, both outdoors and as house plants. *Aucuba* also produces attractive red or yellow berries for which you will need both a male and female plant. *Aucuba japonica* has many cultivars with boldly spotted forms. 'Variegata' has distinct speckled-yellow leaves up to 15cm (6in) long. 'Crotonifolia' has bold golden blotches, and *A. japonica longifolia* has long, bright green, lanceolate leaves.

Aucuba japonica

Brachyglottis repanda

Family: Compositae
Common name: None
Country of origin: New Zealand
Requirement: A position in full sun; frost protection may be required in winter; a good plant for windy or coastal gardens
USDA Zone: Z9

This is a shrub from coastal regions in New Zealand, and is known for its good resistance to wind. It has large attractive grey foliage, white beneath, with leaves growing 10–20cm (4–8in) across, followed by yellow daisy flowers.

Brachyglottis 'Purpurea' has purple leaves with white underneath. This species is for mild, sheltered gardens and will need some protection in colder areas. These shrubs will regenerate from defoliation caused by the cold, often breaking back into growth from shoots at their base.

Brachyglottis repanda

Brugmansia

Family: Solanaceae
Common name: Angel's trumpet
Country of origin: South America
Requirement: A position in full sun or part shade; frost protection is required in winter
USDA Zone: Z9

The wonderfully imposing brugmansias produce pendulous, trumpet-shaped flowers, and large, oblong leaves some 24cm (9in) long and 12cm (5in) wide. They can be grown outside for summer, lifted in autumn and kept in dry, frost-free conditions. Prune in spring to encourage new growth. *Brugmansia arborea* has tubular white flowers, and *B. sanguinea* has orange-yellow tips and yellow-green at the base.

Brugmansia x insignis

Cordyline

Family: Agavaceae
Common name: Cabbage palm
Country of origin: New Zealand
Requirement: Sun or part shade; good for windy or coastal gardens; needs protection against frost in winter
USDA Zone: Z9

The various forms of *Cordyline* are instantly recognizable, with their long, narrow, lanceolate leaves, forming in dense clusters on trunks. There are many different coloured leaf forms and cultivars. The impressive spikes of scented, white flowers arch out in immense plumes.

These plants are best when planted in frost-free temperate gardens or maritime locations. In cold weather the crown of leaves should be tied up into a bunch, to protect the growing point. However, cordylines do have the ability to re-grow from the base should they be severely frosted and defoliated.

Cordyline indivisa is magnificent, and the largest in the family. Its leaves can reach up to 1.5m (5ft) in length and 15cm (6in) across. They are green above, often with red veins and a glaucous grey beneath, giving a very attractive and exotic appearance. This Cordyline can be a little tricky to establish and resents any root movement. Cordylines do not recover from dryness at the root and hate summer drought.

Although not as large as *Cordyline indivisa*, the lesser known C. *kaspar* has broad leaves at up to 10cm (4in) across and 40–100cm (16–36in) long. It's a beauty!

Cordyline kaspar

Cordyline indivisa

Cyphomandra betacea

Family: Solanaceae
Common name: Tamarillo, tree tomato
Country of origin: South America
Requirement: A position in full sun; protect from winter frosts
USDA Zone: Z9

This is a semi-evergreen shrub with heart-shaped leaves up to 25cm (10in) long and 15cm (6in) wide. In its native Peru it grows in forest margins in the tropical highlands of the Andes. It produces small 2.5cm (1in) wide star-shaped flowers that develop into orange-red edible fruits. In cold areas it is best grown in a conservatory. I have had success overwintering it outside in a sheltered corner of the garden under the canopy of evergreen trees where the minimum temperature has been 2°C (34°F).

Cyphomandra betacea

Daphniphyllum himalense var macropodum

Family: Daphniphyllaceae
Common name: None
Country of origin: Japan, Korea, China
Requirement: Grow in a partly shaded site, in a moisture-retentive soil
USDA Zone: Z6

Daphniphyllum makes a rounded shrub to small tree. In its native habitats it enjoys cool and moist, light, open woodland with shelter from drying winds. The preferred soil is a neutral humus-rich loam, although they are quite lime tolerant. The leaves have a wonderful shiny green rhododendron-like appearance, with a contrasting glaucous underside. The young spring growth takes on a pink tinge complemented with the red petioles and midribs. It is hardy to -20°C (-4°F), yet has a really tropical, jungle-like quality.

Daphniphyllum

Entelea arborescens

Family: Tiliaceae
Common name: None
Country of origin: New Zealand
Requirement: A position in full sun or partial shade; frost protection is required in winter
USDA Zone: Z9

This is an attractive shrub or small tree, with large soft hairy leaves 10–15cm (4–6in) long and wide. It produces clusters of small white flowers. It makes a good specimen for the conservatory or cool greenhouse and is very similar in habit and appearance to *Sparmannia africana* (see page 69).

Outside, it requires a warm spot and shelter from cold winds. It grows in any fertile, moist soil. Propagate by cuttings taken in summer.

Entelea arborescens

Euphorbia mellifera

Family: Euphorbiaceae
Common name: Honey spurge
Country of origin: Madeira, Canary Islands
Requirement: Grow in full sun or part shade
USDA Zone: Z8

A medium-sized evergreen sub-shrub to small tree, with narrow oblong leaves up to 20cm (8in), crowned with yellow-brown, honey-scented flowers in spring.

It is not the biggest of foliage plants but makes a good solid shape for structure in the border with an outstanding sub-tropical appearance.

It can survive several degrees of frost.

Euphorbia mellifera

Fatsia japonica

Family: Araliaceae
Common name: Glossy leaved paper plant
Country of origin: Japan
Requirement: Grow in full sun or part shade
USDA Zone: Z8

A familiar plant, it is frequently used in municipal landscapes and public displays, yet it really does have a jungle quality look. The large palmate, polished dark green leaves really can create a sub-tropical effect, or a bold architectural statement.

Fatsia grows well in any warm humid environment with shelter – even near to the sea. It succeeds in part shade or full sun in any moisture-retentive soil and can grow up to 5m (15ft) in height if left to its own devices. It also makes an excellent house or conservatory plant.

In early autumn it produces milky white, globular panicles of flowers on terminal stems held above the bold foliage.

The variegated cultivars are generally considered a little more tender and compact.

Fatsia japonica '*Aurea*'

Fatsia japonica

Fatsia japonica '*Marginata*'

Fuchsia boliviana

Family: Onagraceae
Common name: Lady's eardrops
Country of origin: Argentina, Peru
Requirement: A position in part shade; needs frost protection in winter
USDA Zone: Z10

Fuchsia boliviana makes an upright shrub or small tree. It has large leaves for a fuchsia, up to 15cm (6in) long. The crimson flowers hang down in pendant tubular bell shapes up to 6cm (2½in) long. It needs a warm, mild garden to survive a minimum of -1°C (30°F), so it is best treated as a 'plunged' shrub for the summer border. Lift into pots before the onset of winter, and store under glass. Cut back old wood in the spring to encourage new growth and flowers. If left out over winter the stems can be earthed up, or an extra layer of wood mulch will give some frost protection. *Fuchsia boliviana* var *alba* has white flowers with pink tips to the petals.

Fuchsia boliviana *'Alba'*

Ficus carica

Family: Moraceae
Common name: Common fig
Country of origin: Turkey, Caucasus, Middle East
Requirement: A position in full sun
USDA Zone: Z7

Figs are grown for their fruits yet the beauty of their foliage should not be overlooked. The leaves are quite spectacular, with deep lobes, finger-like and rough to the touch. Preferring a sheltered, warm situation they are actually quite hardy shrubs. They can be fan-trained, although this is more for fruit production. It is possible to grow them as a free-standing shrub.

Ficus carica

Hydrangea

Family: Hydrangeaceae
Common name: None
Country of origin: China
Requirement: A position in partial shade; needs a moisture-retentive soil
USDA Zone: Z7

Hydrangeas are grown primarily for their flowers, yet there are several species that have quite large and attractive leaves. They do well in informal open woodland, thriving in part shade. An acid soil will produce better colour in the flowers.

Hydrangea aspera has narrow and pointed leaves up to 25cm (10in) across, with white to pale pink flowers. *Hydrangea aspera* subsp *sargentiana* is a magnificent plant with tropical-looking leaves 15–25cm (6–10in) across, broadly ovate, and covered in dense hairs. The flowers are pink-white and in lacecap formation.

Hydrangea quercifolia is a loose, rounded shrub, with leaves that are rounded and deeply lobed, like a giant oak leaf.

This selection of hydrangeas can add late summer colour to the garden, and the leaves are big enough to blend in with other exotics without looking out of place.

Hydrangea aspera *subsp* sargentiana

Hydrangea aspera

Ilex perado subsp platyphylla

Family: Aquifoliaceae
Common name: Canary Island holly
Country of origin: Canary Islands
Requirement: A position in full sun or part shade
USDA Zone: Z7

This is quite distinct amongst hollies. Its shiny, ovate evergreen leaves are up to 10cm (4in) wide and 13cm (5in) long, and slightly spiny. It makes a dense shrub to small tree up to 12m (36ft) and is surprisingly hardy. The size of its leaves and imposing form make it an ideal evergreen to create a mainstay of structure in the border, and it is quite happy under the shade of other trees or in full sun.

Ilex perado *subsp* platyphylla

Isoplexis sceptrum

Family: Scrophulariaceae
Common name: Foxglove shrub
Country of origin: Madeira
Requirement: Position in full sun or part shade; protect from frost in winter
USDA Zone: Z9

This evergreen sub-shrub grows up to 2m (6ft) with ovate-oblong leaves, 10–25cm (4–10in) long and hairy beneath. It occurs naturally in the mountainous laurel forests of Madeira, requiring well-drained soil, shelter, and a sunny to partially shaded site. The bold foliage is topped by dense spikes of orange-tawny foxglove-shaped flowers. It looks spectacular when planted en masse.

Isoplexis sceptrum

Melianthus major

Family: Melianthaceae
Common name: Honey flower
Country of origin: South Africa
Requirement: A position in full sun or part shade
USDA Zone: Z8

Melianthus is a robust sub-shrub with blue-grey jagged foliage, followed by spikes of upright dark chocolate-coloured flowers. They form into inflated fruit capsules, which hang on for some time, adding to the interest. In frosty weather the plant can be cut to the ground, but if it is planted a little deeper than normal, this helps protect the stem, and vigorous regrowth will take place in the spring. Mulching with leaf litter, bracken or woodchip also protects the roots. Poor soils with less available nutrients seem to promote better flowering.

Melianthus major *with seed capsules*

Metapanax davidii

Family: Araliaceae
Common name: None
Country of origin: N. Vietnam, China
Requirement: A position in full sun or part shade
USDA Zone: Z7

These are bushy evergreen shrubs with similar habit and appearance to *Pseudopanax*. The 15cm (6in) long leaves are curiously shaped, often trilobed, whilst some remain entire or undivided. They are best suited to the dappled light conditions of the woodland edge, in half-shade to full sun. The flowers are green-yellow umbels as much as 18cm (7in) across, followed by black fleshy seeds or fruit to 6mm ($^1/_4$in) wide.

Metapanax davidii

Paulownia tomentosa

Family: Scrophulariaceae
Common name: Foxglove tree
Country of origin: China
Requirement: A position in full sun or part shade
USDA Zone: Z5

If left to grow normally, *Paulownia* makes a handsome tree with large leaves and a broad crown, topped with lilac foxglove-shaped flowers. Young plants should be severely pruned to the ground in spring, and the resultant suckers are then thinned out to leave one single shoot. This shoot can grow to 3m (10ft) in one season and produce enormous leaves up to 80cm (32in) across. This is known as 'stooling', and the overall effect is to produce giant leaves that are imposing and tropical looking. This is particularly useful for an exotic-style garden in a cold site where some reliable permanent structure plants are needed.

Paulownias are quite hardy, except that their flowers are prone to frost damage.

Paulownia tomentosa

Phormium

Family: Phormiaceae
Common name: Flax
Country of origin: New Zealand
Requirement: A position in full sun; needs a moisture-retentive soil; a good plant for coastal gardens
USDA Zone: Z8

These shrubby perennials have handsome evergreen swordlike leaves, and make architectural and striking plants in any garden situation. They thrive in coastal conditions or exposed sites and grow in a variety of soils.

Forms of *Phormium tenax* make the biggest, stiff upright clumps with tough leathery leaves up to 3m (10ft), usually forked at the tip, and massively tall flower spikes to 4m (14ft). *Phormium cookianum* has slightly softer and lax leaves.

There are many fine coloured leaf cultivars and hybrids between the two species. Some are prone to reverting back to the plain green of one of the parents. At the first signs of this you can pull that section away from the main crown to keep it true to the coloured form. In mild, damp summers the crown can get infected by the mealy bug pest.

A site with better air flow helps reduce infection. Regular spraying with an approved insecticide will be needed for heavy infestation.

Phormium cookianum *'Cream Delight'*

Phormium cookianum *'Jester'*

Phormium tenax

Pittosporum

Family: Pittosporaceae
Common name: None
Country of origin: Australasia, East and South-East Asia
Requirement: Full sun or partial shade
USDA Zone: Z8

Pittosporum is a large genus of evergreen shrubs to small trees, mostly suited to mild maritime areas. The foliage is often used in the floristry industry. The largest leaved of all the species is *Pittosporum daphniphylloides*. Its large 25cm (10in) long leaves are ovate to oblanceolate, dark green and glossy. Complemented with creamy, scented flowers in terminal clusters from late spring to mid-summer. They are reasonably hardy in a sheltered garden and seem quite happy in light woodland canopy, or in full sun with good drainage.

Pittosporum eugenioides 'Platinum' is an attractive variegated shrub with a unique, almost metallic sheen to the 15cm (6in) long leaves held on black stems.

Pittosporum eugenioides *'Platinum'*

Pittosporum daphniphylloides

Prunus laurocerasus 'Castlewellan'

Family: Rosaceae
Common name: Cherry laurel
Country of origin: Eastern Europe
Requirement: A position in partial shade
USDA Zone: Z7

This shrub may still be found under its old name of 'Marbled White'. *Prunus* may seem an odd choice for the tropical look, but the reasonably large evergreen leaves of this form are spectacularly marbled throughout with white freckles. This has a startling effect when used as a foil plant, or to light up a shady corner. The leaves also have a resemblance to the tropical *Croton* foliage plants, yet here is a plant that is hardy enough for Zone 7.

Prunus laurocerasus *'Castlewellan'*

Pseudopanax

Family: Araliaceae
Common name: Lancewoods
Country of origin: New Zealand
Requirement: A position in full sun or partial shade; protect from frost in winter
USDA Zone: Z9

These are shrubs to small trees with interesting, glossy evergreen leaves that are quite thick, leathery and often toothed. They make wonderful structure plants and have quite a jungle-like appearance. They are tolerant of shade and full sun, but prefer a sheltered position in a mild maritime garden. They grow in any fertile, well-drained soil.

In really cold areas they are best grown in containers and either stood in a sheltered spot, or plunged, and then overwintered in a cool conservatory or glasshouse.

Pseudopanax laetus has some of the largest leaves, up to 25cm (10in) long, with small, dark purple to black flowers in terminal umbels.

Pseudopanax arboreus

Pseudopanax laetus

Pseudopanax x 'Cyril Watson'

Schefflera

Family: Araliaceae
Common name: Umbrella tree
Country of origin: Asia, Australasia, South Africa
Requirement: A position in full sun or part shade; protect from frost in winter
USDA Zone: Z9/Z10

Many people will be familiar with the sub-tropical house plant known as the umbrella tree (*Schefflera actinophylla*) with its finger-like, radiating leaflets. It is, of course, quite tender, but there are other species that are proving to be tougher than expected. *Schefflera delavayi* and *Schefflera taiwenensis* are known to be growing outside in sheltered gardens in the far south-west of the UK. They have similar, irregularly lobed leaflets up to 25cm (10in) long and 14cm (5$\frac{1}{2}$in) wide, and still retain an exotic appearance. Cold winds and frost will defoliate them, so during particularly chilly times it is recommended that you wrap them in a fleece or hessian sacking, and the roots will need a deep organic mulch.

Schefflera can grow outdoors in a sheltered garden

Solanum laciniatum

Family: Solanaceae
Common name: Kangaroo apple
Country of origin: Australia, New Zealand
Requirement: A position in full sun or part shade; protect from frost in winter
USDA Zone: Z9

This plant makes an unusual evergreen shrub up to 3m (10ft) tall, with variable, deeply divided foliage and leaves up to 30cm (12in) long. The indigo flowers are followed by showy oval green to yellow fruit. Often found growing on open scrubland, it is happy in any fertile soil. In colder climates it will need a warm site, such as at the base of a wall. A thick layer of mulch will be needed to protect the rootstock. Once established, the seed appears to be spread by birds, and seedlings can occur around the garden. The devil's fig (*Solanum hispidum*) and white-margined nightshade (*Solanum marginatum*) may be difficult to find, but would also be worth a try as they have large tropical-looking leaves. Although some textbooks quote a winter minimum of 5°C (41°F), I suspect given a really sheltered site they may be all right in Zone 9.

Solanum laciniatum

Sparmannia africana

Family: Tiliaceae
Common name: Zimmerlinden
Country of origin: South Africa
Requirement: Full sun; winter frost protection is required
USDA Zone: Z10

An attractive and imposing shrub with ovate leaves up to 25cm (10in) long, that are irregularly toothed, rough and hairy to touch. The flowers are in small white clusters with purple stamens. In cooler zones they make excellent container plants for the patio, or can even be plunged outside in a sheltered sunny border for the summer.

Propagate from seed, cuttings or layering.

Sparmannia africana

Telanthophora grandifolia

Family: Compositae
Common name: None
Country of origin: Mexico
Requirement: A position in full sun or part shade; protect from frost in winter
USDA Zone: Z10

A small shrub to 2m (6ft) with large leaves up to 20cm (8in) across, crowned with big heads of yellow mopheaded flowers formed from ray florets. Being tender it is suited to the cool conservatory, but will make a bold exotic specimen in the border of a sheltered and mild garden with well-drained soil.

Telanthophora grandifolia

Tetrapanax papyrifer

Family: Araliaceae
Common name: Chinese rice-paper plant
Country of origin: Taiwan
Requirement: A position in full sun or part shade; protect from frost in winter
USDA Zone: Z8

Tetrapanax is one of the most spectacular of shrubs, with huge lobed, umbrella-like leaves up to 50cm (20in) or more across. There are several different leaf forms of this plant, differing mainly in the size and shape of the lobes. In Asia the white stem pith is a major source for fine rice-paper. In Taiwan it grows in sub-tropical forests, where it creates a thicket from its running suckers. Open-grown plants in colder environments may be frosted to the ground, but they often regenerate from the roots in the spring. Annual hard pruning will keep the plant bushier and encourage larger leaves. Keep the roots well mulched and water well in the summer.

Tetrapanax papyrifer

Trevesia palmata

Family: Araliaceae
Common name: Snowflake tree
Country of origin: Himalayas, Indo-China, Vietnam
Requirement: A sheltered position in damp, partial shade; protect from frost in winter
USDA Zone: Z10

This prickly species has large palmate leaves to 60cm (2ft) across. The dark green and glossy juvenile leaves have distinct pseudo-leaflets that add to its rather unusual complex leaf shape. Regular pruning will encourage this spectacular growth, which is often used in the floristry industry. These plants generally grow in damp, sheltered, shady woodland. The species can be variable, which has led to two varieties being named 'Micholitzii' and 'Sanderi', but these will be hard to find.

Trevesia palmata

Vasconcella quercifolia

Family: Caricaceae
Common name: Mountain pawpaw
Country of origin: South America, Andean highlands
Requirement: A position in full sun or part shade; protect from frost in winter
USDA Zone: Z9

This is the shrublike highland species of the pawpaw, valued in the tropics for its fruits. It is slightly more cold tolerant than *Carica papaya*, the commercial pawpaw, and will grow in cooler temperate zones where it makes an attractive foliage plant with deeply lobed leaves up to 30cm (12in) long. Grow in a sheltered position where it might survive -5°C (23°F). Fruit appears if both male and female plants are grown. Keep the plants dry in winter.

Vasconcella quercifolia

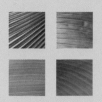

Large-leaved trees A-Z

I n the last chapter we looked at shrubs and some of the trees that are at home in smaller gardens. Here, we will see some of the larger-growing trees that also have some fabulous dramatic leaves. As before, some may be hard to find, but they are all worth the search.

Acer franchetii

Family: Aceraceae
Common name: Franchets' maple
Country of origin: China
Requirement: A position in full sun or partial shade; needs a moisture-retentive soil
USDA Zone: Z6

This tree will grow up to 7m (23ft), and is quite slow-growing. It has attractive, large, three-lobed leaves with the base slightly heart-shaped, 7.5–20cm (3–8in) long and wide, on long leaf stalks. The leaf veining can be highlighted with the sun shining through them.

It is a deciduous tree, and grows best in full sun to dappled shade in moisture-retentive soils. On account of its generous leaf size, it would be worthy of a place in a woody jungle-like planting.

Acer franchetii

Ailanthus altissima

Family: Simaroubaceae
Common name: Tree of Heaven
Country of origin: China
Requirement: Full sun or partial shade
USDA Zone: Z7

This is a particularly fine tree when mature, with an attractive grey bark and large pinnate leaves that emerge in the spring with a pink-red hue to them. It produces large, handsome clusters of reddish-brown single-seeded fruits. It is a fast grower and tolerant of a wide range of growing conditions.

For tropical effect and the finest foliage, it is best cut to the ground in the spring, then allow a single shoot to regrow.

Ailanthus altissima

Aralia elata 'Aureovariegata'

Family: Araliaceae
Common name: Japanese angelica tree
Country of origin: Japan
Requirement: A position in full sun; needs a moisture-retentive soil
USDA Zone: Z4

The angelica tree makes a small tree or suckering shrub, preferring a sheltered site in well-drained but moisture-retentive soil.

Its huge double pinnate leaves are particularly attractive with the cultivar 'Aureovariegata', with leaflets coloured white to yellow on the margins. However, this variegated form is less vigorous and should be grafted on to the straight green *Aralia elata* to give it vigour.

Flowers are formed in large white panicles in late summer.

Grow this tree as a backdrop for brightly coloured *Canna*; the *Aralia* leaves make a good foil.

Aralia elata *'Aureovariegata'*

Catalpa

Family: Bignoniaceae
Common name: Indian bean tree
Country of origin: North America, China
Requirement: A position in full sun; needs a moisture-retentive soil
USDA Zone: Z5

Catalpa is a beautiful late-summer-flowering deciduous tree, with large handsome leaves. It requires a moisture-retentive fertile soil in a sunny spot, and a sheltered site to prevent its foliage from being shredded in the wind.

It can also be cut back hard in the spring or 'stooled' for greater foliage effect. *Catalpa* x *erubescens* 'Purpurea' has very dark purple foliage in the spring, turning dark green later. It makes a good foil for *Canna*, or the white seed headed grasses such as *Stipa*, perennials such as *Kniphofia*, or the vivid, rich orange of annuals such as *Tithonia*.

Catalpa bignonioides *'Aurea'*

Catalpa bignonioides *'Variegata'*

Catalpa erubescens *'Purpurea'*

Eriobotrya japonica

Family: Rosaceae
Common name: Loquat, Japanese medlar
Country of origin: China, Japan
Requirement: A position in full sun or partial shade
USDA Zone: Z7

The loquat makes an attractive shrub to small tree, with large dark evergreen corrugated leaves up to 30cm (12in) long. It is prized for its ornamental and architectural form, and can make a good backbone and structure plant for a sheltered garden. In true sub-tropical climates it is grown for its globular edible fruits, but in the UK it only produces clusters of white flowers and yellow fruits after long hot summers. In Japan there are over 800 different varieties in cultivation.

Eriobotrya japonica

Eucalyptus nitens

Family: Myrtaceae
Common name: Silver top gum tree
Country of origin: Australia
Requirement: A site in full sun or partial shade
USDA Zone: Z8

The *Eucalyptus* family is large and diverse with trees growing in a wide range of conditions. For the sub-tropical effect *Eucalyptus nitens* makes a wonderful backdrop if you have the space, as it can get quite big if not pollarded or stooled at an early age. Its leaves are long and ribbon-like, with a silver sheen, and even more attractive at the juvenile stage when they take on a coppery tinge. The Tasmanian blue gum (*E. globulus*) with large blue-green leaves is another species for the mild garden. Both trees make better specimens in a sheltered, warm site.

Juvenile foliage of Eucalyptus

Firmiana simplex

Family: Sterculiaceae
Common name: Chinese parasol tree
Country of origin: Eastern Asia
Requirement: A position in full sun or part shade; protect from frost in winter
USDA Zone: Z9

This is an attractive deciduous-foliage tree with large, shiny 40cm (16in) wide maple-like leaves. In warmer countries it is grown as a shade tree, but in cooler climates it will need shelter and winter protection if it is to thrive. Making a large shrub to small tree, it requires plenty of summer warmth to put on strong growth.

It can also be grown as a specimen container plant where it could overwinter under glass and be plunged outside for the summer.

Firmiana simplex

Idesia polycarpa

Family: Flacourtiaceae
Common name: None
Country of origin: Japan, China
Requirement: A site in full sun or partial shade
USDA Zone: Z5

This small tree from mountainous areas 2,000m (9,842ft) or more high, has large attractive heart-shaped leaves, 20cm (8in) long and 24cm (10in) wide, glaucous beneath and very ornamental. The small yellow-green pendulous flowers are followed by bunches of pea-like red berries. It is quite hardy and prefers an acid soil with a deep loam. Its appearance does give a tropical jungle look and it would make a good structure plant in the mixed exotic border.

Idesia polycarpa

Itoa orientalis

Family: Flacourtiaceae
Common name: None
Country of origin: Vietnam
Requirement: Full sun or partial shade
USDA Zone: Z8

This unusual tree from Vietnam has large oval leaves resembling *Magnolia*. It makes a small slow-growing specimen in cooler climates and seems to do well in an open, sheltered site with a deep moisture-retentive soil. It has been known to survive -6°C (21°F), with only a limited amount of defoliation. It is well worth growing for its exotic-looking foliage.

Itoa orientalis

Liriodendron chinense

Family: Magnoliaceae
Common name: Chinese tulip tree
Country of origin: N. Vietnam, China
Requirement: A position in full sun, and a moisture-retentive soil
USDA Zone: Z7

This is the smaller cousin to the North American tulip tree (*Liriodendron tulipifera*). It is the curiously shaped, deeply three-lobed leaves that catch the eye and could easily be a substitute for an exotic counterpart. The flowers are smaller, green, and not so attractive as *L. tulipifera*. It likes a deep, fertile soil where it can be quite a fast grower.

Liriodendron chinense

Magnolia

Family: Magnoliaceae
Common name: None
Country of origin: Japan, China, Himalayas, North-East America, tropical America
Requirement: A position in partial shade and a moisture retentive soil
USDA Zone: Various

Magnolias are some of the most magnificent of hardy flowering trees to be grown in temperate zones, and the exquisite, scented flowers are immediately recognizable. Yet many of these trees possess exceptionally large and attractive foliage that would not look out of place in the exotic environment.

Most are from high altitudes and prefer moisture-retentive, humus-rich soils, and a sheltered woodland-type location.

Good examples include *Magnolia delavayi* (Z9), with some of the largest evergreen leaves up to 30cm (12in) long. *Magnolia macrophylla* (Z6) has some of the largest deciduous leaves in the UK, and *Magnolia officinalis* var *biloba* (Z8) is a rare and quite distinct Chinese species with leaves up to 40cm (16in) long. *Magnolia tripetala* is also a good hardy North American species with wonderfully large leaves 30–50cm (12–20cm) long, together with cream-coloured flowers and cone-shaped fruiting clusters.

Magnolia macrophylla

Magnolia delavayi

Magnolia officinalis *var* biloba

Populus lasiocarpa

Family: Salicaceae
Common name: Chinese necklace popular
Country of origin: South-West China
Requirement: A position in full sun, and a moisture retentive soil
USDA Zone: Z5

A magnificent, hardy, medium-sized tree, which has attractive 30cm (12in) long and 25cm (10in) wide leaves with red veining and red leaf stalks. It prefers a sheltered site. Annual pruning will keep it in scale for a smaller garden and help it to produce its large and attractive foliage. It does have quite a greedy and extensive root system, and it also produces a lot of seed 'cotton' debris.

Populus lasiocarpa

Rhododendron

Family: Ericaceae
Common name: None
Country of origin: Scattered throughout temperate regions in the northern and southern hemispheres, particularly Asia, South-West China, Burma, India and Papua New Guinea
Requirement: Partial shade and a moisture-retentive soil
USDA Zone: Various

The *Rhododendron* is one of the largest and most diverse groups of plants, known primarily for its stunning flowers and handsome foliage. It may not be an immediate choice as an exotic-looking tree or large shrub, but it can complement a sub-tropical planting style, as there are many species with big, bold evergreen leaves. A semi-shaded and sheltered site with a moisture-retentive acid soil suits most of the large-leaved species. The following are some of the better ones to look out for: *Rhododenron basilicum, R. calophytum, R. falconeri, R. macabeanum, R. magnificum, R. montroseanum* and *R. sinogrande*.

Rhododendron sinogrande

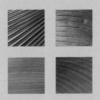

Palms and cycads A-Z

Of all the picturesque images of the tropics it is the majestic palm tree that overrides my thoughts, with its giant feathery leaves on tall flexing trunks. The good news is that not all palm trees are frost-tender and from the tropics. There are several species that will make impressively bold specimens for the exotic-looking garden, even in colder climates.

This chapter will deal with some of the proven palms that I have found to be particularly effective for the temperate garden, although there is plenty of scope for further trials with other species that could prove hardy. For example, the Mazari palm (*Nannorrhops ritchieana*) is an arid desert palm from the Middle East, Afghanistan and Pakistan, yet it is extremely cold-tolerant and will survive under snow for long periods of the winter. Unfortunately it is quite rare in cultivation, and therefore difficult to find.

Brahea

Family: Palmae – Arecaceae
Common name: Hesper palm
Country of origin: Central America, Mexico, Baja California
Requirement: A position in full sun
USDA Zone: Z9

This palm species is highly adaptable, succeeding in temperate and tropical zones, often growing in colonies on poor, rocky ground. It succeeds best in full sun but will not tolerate poor drainage.

Brahea armata is proving to be quite hardy in the more favourable climates in the UK, but it is slow-growing, producing only one or two new stiff, blue-green leaves a year. If you garden in a temperate climate, buy the largest specimen you can afford for instant impact. The rock palm (*Brahea dulcis*) from Mexico has attractive fan-shaped leaves, and finally there is *Brahea edulis*, which also makes a fine ornamental specimen once established.

Brahea armata *grown in a container*

A mature, free-standing Brahea armata

Butia capitata

Family: Palmae – Arecaceae
Common name: Wine palm
Country of origin: South America
Requirement: A position in full sun
USDA Zone: Z8

Butia capitata has distinct arching bluish-green fronds up to 80cm (32in) long. It is slow-growing yet will make a distinctive woody trunk up to 5m (16ft) in time. The palm will tolerate several degrees of frost but not weeks of frozen ground. It hates wet, poorly drained soil so good drainage with full sun is vital. However, in the height of summer it is important to keep the roots well watered. *Butia yatay* from Argentina also makes a handsome palm and is well worth trying. In the wild both forms grow in quite dry sandy soils.

Palms *at Isola Bella, Lake Maggiore, Italy*

Chamaerops humilis

Family: Palmae – Arecaceae
Common name: European fan palm
Country of origin: Southern Europe, North Africa
Requirement: A position in full sun
USDA Zone: Z7

One of the toughest palms, it grows well in temperate regions. Some forms make dense clumps with several stout trunks, others remain compact with dense foliage as with the cultivar 'Green Mound'. The blue-green leaves have sharp-spined leaf petioles, so take care when weeding close up. These palms are quite drought-resistant and grow in a wide range of soils. As an accent plant they make excellent focal points for island beds, and also grow well as containerized specimens.

The blue chamaerops (C. *humilis* var *cerifera*) comes from the high Atlas Mountains of Morocco and, as its common name suggests, has quite distinct blue-green leaves.

Chamaerops humilis

Chamaerops humilis *var* cerifera

Jubaea chilensis

Family: Palmae – Arecaceae
Common name: Chilean wine palm
Country of origin: Chile
Requirement: A position in full sun
USDA Zone: Z7

The Jubaea palm produces a sweet sugary sap from which the locals make delicacies called palm honey and palm wine.

The palm produces a massive trunk and a broad spreading crown, and is popular as an accent plant for parks or private driveways. These plants are quite frost-tolerant but slow-growing at first, speeding up once the roots and trunk have really established. They require a sunny well-drained position.

Jubaea chilensis

Livistona chinensis

Family: Palmae – Arecaceae
Common name: Fountain palm
Country of origin: Southern China, Taiwan
Requirement: A position in full sun; needs frost protection in winter
USDA Zone: Z10

This palm is often seen as an indoor specimen in temperate parts of the world, yet it can grow outside in mild gardens, and can even take short spells of frost. Its leaves have a soft yellow-green lustre and have weeping leaf tips.

It is slow-growing in cooler climates and prefers a site in full sun, yet it can do well in shade. Water well in dry weather and provide a thick mulch with insulated covering for prolonged periods of cold weather.

Phoenix canariensis

Family: Palmae – Arecaceae
Common name: Canary Island date palm
Country of origin: Canary Islands
Requirement: A position in full sun
USDA Zone: Z8

This is one of the most widely grown palms in the world. It has proven to be very adaptable at growing in various climates, proving to be quite frost-resistant and thriving in poor soils, as long as there is adequate drainage.

The light green fronds are pinnate and have sharp spiny leaflets at their bases. Given plenty of well-rotted manure and slow release organic bonemeal fertilizer, they will establish quite quickly, although they take many years to produce the tall woody trunks that are their trademark in the tropics.

Young plantation of Phoenix canariensis *at Abbotsbury*

Mature *Phoenix canariensis* at Tresco Abbey Gardens, Isles of Scilly, Cornwall, England

Rhapidophyllum hystrix

Family: Palmae – Arecaceae
Common name: Needle palm
Country of origin: South-Eastern United States
Requirement: A position in full sun or part shade
USDA Zone: Z7

A clump-forming, slow-growing palm with large palmate leaves up to 1m (3ft) across. The trunks are covered in black spines emanating from the leaf sheaths. It is increasingly rare in the wild where it succeeds in humus-rich woodlands, in shade to full sun.

Rhapis excelsa

Family: Palmae – Arecaceae
Common name: Lady palm
Country of origin: Southern China
Requirement: A position in full sun or part shade
USDA Zone: Z9

This is one of the best palms for growing indoors in containers, and will even tolerate a certain amount of neglect and poor light levels. It produces multi-stemmed trunks covered with woven brown fibre. For temperate regions it is worth trying outside as it seems to be quite cold-tolerant. It is best in a semi-protected site with half-shade, such as under the canopies of taller trees. It is slow-growing, so provide a good mulch and keep it well watered.

Rhapis excelsa

Sabal minor

Family: Palmae – Arecaceae
Common name: Dwarf palmetto palm
Country of origin: South-Eastern United States
Requirement: A position in full sun, in a moisture-retentive soil
USDA Zone: Z9

This palm has a subterranean trunk with stiff blue leaves rising at the surface to form a crown. It can form an impressive above-ground trunk up to 15m (49ft) tall, with a large crown of palmate leaves, followed by a long, spherical inflorescence producing 20mm ($^3/_4$in) long black fruit. It occurs in the wild in the Rio Grande river valley of southern Texas, and as a common palm species of the lowland tropical parts of Mexico.

It is cold-hardy, requiring full sun, and preferring moist ground; in its native habitat it grows in alluvial floodplains and swamps. It is a useful palm at the front of a planting scheme where its low-growing shape will not dominate.

Sabal mexicana is also hardy, and thrives in hot, dry climates from tropical to temperate.

Trachycarpus

Family: Palmae – Arecaceae
Common name: Chusan palm, Chinese windmill palm
Country of origin: China
Requirement: A position in full sun or part shade
USDA Zone: Z7

Trachycarpus fortunei was named after Robert Fortune, the 19th-century plant hunter. It is a very cold-hardy palm, and grown for its fan-shaped leaves and hairy trunk. From the leafy crown it produces attractive yellow clumps of flowering inflorescence.

There is another attractive form called *T. wagnerianus* with smaller, stiffer leaves, yet it is not known in the wild and is probably not a distinct species. *T. nanus* is a dwarf species and *T. takil* is another form without the woolly trunk of *T. fortunei*.

A much more distinct species and slightly less hardy is *T. martianus*, with typical fan-shaped, glossy leaves, yet only divided about halfway. The trunk is slim, bare and ringed. For the cool temperate exotic garden there is no better palm for creating a framework, an impressive avenue, or for a solitary architectural specimen.

All *Trachycarpus* like an open, sunny situation and need good drainage.

(Photographs overleaf)

91

Trachycarpus fortunei

Trachycarpus martianus

Trithrinax campestris

Family: Palmae – Arecaceae
Common name: Carunday palm
Country of origin: Argentina, Brazil
Requirement: A position in full sun
USDA Zone: Z9

This is a handsome multi-stemmed palm, with stiff, spiny, fan-shaped leaves. It is slow-growing and could prove to be reasonably hardy. Plant in full sun with free-draining soil (it is tolerant of dry conditions). Avoid planting too close to the edge of the border where the sharp spines on the leaves could cause damage. This palm is comparatively rare in cultivation.

Trithrinax campestris

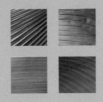

Cycads

For sheer drama and tropical effect, cycads must be near the top of the 'must-have' list. They have colonized the earth since prehistoric times and are now only found in the wild in some of the more remote warm and humid regions.

They are palm-like, with stiff pinnate leaves in terminal crowns above woody trunks. Nearly all require tropical conditions with a minimum of 12°C (54°F), with one exception – *Cycas revoluta*.

Cycas revoluta

Family: Cycadaceae
Common name: Sago palm
Country of origin: Japan
Requirement: A position in full sun or part shade
USDA Zone: Z9

This small palm-like cycad is the most widely known and probably the hardiest. Growing them outside in more temperate gardens can be quite a challenge and even a dilemma, as they are expensive plants to buy and one doesn't want to risk losing too many of them to the rigours of a cold winter. They can take temperatures of -5°C (23°F) for short periods, such as in Mediterranean climates, but to be pragmatic they are best grown in suitable containers which can be brought in under frost-free glass for the winter.

The pinnate leaves are semi-rigid, glossy and dark green but can be prone to scale insect or mealy bug infestations. If this occurs it is best to treat them by wiping the leaves clean with a rag soaked in metholated spirits, as they can have a phytotoxic reaction with other chemicals.

Cycas revoluta

Ferns A-Z

Ferns are found growing in all types of climates around the world and are renowned for their fine and varied foliage forms.

As with the fern boom of the Victorian era, the upsurge in popularity in recent times has given them a higher profile at garden centres, especially the soft tree fern (*Dicksonia antarctica*). This is one plant that can create instant impact and a foreign flavour when grown in the right conditions and chosen locality.

Gardeners with temperate or sub-tropical gardens who are stylising the garden for the 'exotic look' should choose ferns with large fronds, preferably evergreen, and plant them in natural-looking groups or drifts. This chapter deals with a proven selection of plants that have the right effect; most are hardy, with the odd exception needing tender loving care.

Asplenium nidus

Family: Aspleniaceae
Common name: Bird's nest fern
Country of origin: Tropical regions
Requirement: A position in part shade, in a moisture-retentive soil; protect from frost in winter
USDA Zone: Z10

This is one of the best known tropical ferns and is widely available. It is not an ideal candidate for the temperate garden as it is totally tropical requiring warm and humid conditions. Yet there may be some maritime gardens with a favoured climate that could sustain this luscious plant outside in pots or tubs for short periods of summer before returning them to the conservatory or glasshouse. They grow with a spectacular spreading rosette of fronds, in the wild individually up to 1.5m (5ft) long and 20cm (8in) wide. This fern is often epiphytic, growing successfully without soil, on damp tree branches, rock faces and boulders.

Asplenium nidus

Athyrium nipponicum

Family: Dryopteridaceae
Common name: None
Country of origin: North East Asia
Requirement: A position in partial shade, and a moisture-retentive soil
USDA Zone: Z4

In the wild this species grows in moist, sheltered damp woodland, with an acid soil and lots of leaf mould. The form known as *Athyrium nipponicum* var *pictum* has particularly attractive young fronds with a purple-pink midrib or veining showing through the almost metallic-grey to aquamarine-green leaves. This is a useful plant for a shady corner where the subtle colouring of the fronds can be used to link in with other plants in the border.

Athyrium nipponicum *var* pictum

Blechnum chilense

Family: Blechnaceae
Common name: Hard fern
Country of origin: South America
Requirement: A position in full sun or part shade; needs a moisture-retentive soil
USDA Zone: Z7

An excellent colonizer, this fern will slowly spread as an exotic-looking evergreen ground cover if there is an abundance of moisture. It grows in sun or shade and is easy to propagate by division. Its pinnate fronds can get to 90cm (36in) long, and they look quite spectacular in large drifts.

It naturally blends into the landscape, especially when grown in or near a water feature, such as a streamside. The colourful new fronds make an attractive feature in the springtime.

This plant mostly prefers an acid soil, with plenty of organic mulch around the crown and root zone.

Blechnum chilense

Dicksonia

Family: Dicksoniaceae
Common name: Soft tree fern
Country of origin: New Zealand, Tasmania, Australia
Requirement: A position in full sun or part shade; needs a moisture-retentive soil
USDA Zone: Z9

Tree ferns are really impressive as specimen plants with their huge green fronds to 2m (6ft) long and 90cm (3ft) wide. The hairy trunks, 1–3m (3–10ft) tall, are made up of matted roots, looking rather like coconut matting.

These ferns require semi-shade, moisture, good humidity, and preferably a sheltered site to protect their brittle fronds. In cooler temperate gardens they will take several degrees of frost for short periods. Protect the crowns with dead bracken or even wrap the trunks with old carpet for protection if a cold spell is forecast. In dry conditions it is important to water the trunks to encourage root growth through the stem.

Dicksonia antarctica, *D. fibrosa* and *D. squarrosa* are the most reliable for cooler climates.

Another tree fern genus that is worth trying outside if you have a very favourable microclimate is *Cyathea*. There are several interesting species, such as *C. dealbata* with silvery white undersides to the fronds, and *C. medullaris* with splendid black scales. However, they can be tricky to establish.

Dicksonia antarctica

Dicksonia fibrosa

Dicksonia squarrosa

Dryopteris wallichiana

Family: Dryopteridaceae
Common name: None
Country of origin: Asia, South America, Africa
Requirement: A position in part shade, in a moisture-retentive soil
USDA Zone: Z6

These ferns form an imposing open tussock, producing wonderful unfurling fronds with black scales in spring. They are from mountainous regions, growing in cool shade and acid soil with plenty of organic leaf mould. They are hardy down to -21°C (-4°F).

Dryopteris wallichiana

Lophosoria quadripinnata

Family: Lophosoriaceae
Common name: Tree fern
Country of origin: Central and South America, Mexico
Requirement: A position in part shade, in a moisture-retentive soil
USDA Zone: Z9

This tree fern is distributed throughout Central America, from Mexico to Chile. It thrives in mild, damp woodland. It is slow-growing, and eventually forms a trunk up to 1m (3ft) in height, with large fronds to 4m (13ft), that have glaucous undersides and pale brown rhizomes covered in dense hairs. It is wonderfully jungle-like, yet not often seen in cultivation. You may have difficulty in locating specimens to purchase. This is surprising really, when they have been known in the wild to take several degrees of frost. It should do well in mild, sheltered temperate gardens, with an acid soil and lots of rich leaf mould.

Todea barbara

Family: Osmundaceae
Common name: Austral king fern
Country of origin: New Zealand, Australia, South Africa
Requirement: A position in partial shade, and a moisture-retentive soil; needs frost protection in winter
USDA Zone: Z10

This is a real tropical rainforest fern for a warm site with shady moist areas, although it is quite adaptable in gardens and can also be grown as a container specimen. In time it can develop multiple crowns with a black fibrous trunk. The bright green fronds are upright and leathery, like a small tree fern. Choose a sheltered area under the protection of trees and provide a deep organic mulch around the crown before winter. They will need glasshouse protection in cold winter areas.

Todea barbara

Woodwardia radicans

Family: Blechnaceae
Common name: Chain fern
Country of origin: Europe, Asia
Requirement: A position in partial shade, in a moisture-retentive soil
USDA Zone: Z9

These are ferns suited to high humidity, so a moist soil or streamside planting is ideal, or a border soil with plenty of organic matter at the roots. *Woodwardia radicans* produces graceful fronds up to 2m (6ft), emerging with red growth in the spring. They propagate with plantlets that grow from the tips of the fronds.

As a big fern, it needs space, where it can slowly colonize. Some winter protection may be needed in really cold spells.

The enormous leaves have a hint of the tropics, and make an excellent contrast to the leaves of such plants as the Japanese banana.

Woodwardia radicans

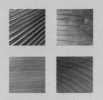

Bananas and closely related plants A-Z

This group of plants must surely be the most influential and tropical-looking of all the architectural impact foliage plants. The giant paddle-shaped leaves of *Musa* are instantly recognizable as those of the tropical banana fruit, of which there are about 50 species and several hybrids. For temperate gardens the choice is rather more limited, yet there are several species that are proving to be reliably hardy for Zones 8 and 9. Of course, there are many species such as *Ensete*, that can be grown as containerized plants and 'plunged' for the summer months.

Ensete

Family: Musaceae
Common name: None
Country of origin: Africa, Asia
Requirement: A position in full sun, in a moisture-retentive soil; needs frost protection in winter
USDA Zone: Z10

Often assumed to be a banana, *Ensete* is closely related with enormous paddle-shaped leaves, but it does not produce suckers ('pups') as with the true banana genus (*Musa*). *Ensete* generally requires full sun, and good shelter to prevent the massive 2–6m (6–20ft) long leaves from becoming shredded and tatty in the wind. During the growing season these plants require regular watering and a liquid feed to encourage continuous growth. They can only take a light ground frost for a short length of time, so they are best dug up and containerized before the onset of winter, or in extremely mild gardens the crown can be protected with bracken fronds or other insulation, and left in situ.

Ensete glaucum is a high altitude species from Yunnan that could prove to be quite cold-tolerant. It has a distinct glaucous-green trunk, and blue-green leaves to 2m (6ft) in length.

Ensete ventricosum is an important crop in certain parts of Africa. It was a favourite with Victorians for summer bedding schemes. It makes a huge plant in time. *Ensete ventricosum* 'Maurelii' has an unusual richly coloured leaf of suffused red and black, making a wonderful foil to work with when colour designing with plants in the sub-tropical garden. All Ensetes can be container grown if space is restrictive, but do not allow them to dry out at the root.

Ensete glaucum

Ensete ventricosum *'Maurelii'*

Ensete ventricosum

Musa

Family: Musaceae
Common name: Banana
Country of origin: Asia
Requirement: A position in full sun or partial shade; needs a moisture-retentive soil
USDA Zone: Z8

Bananas are known worldwide for their tropical fruits, and are grown in vast areas of the tropics. There are about 50 naturally occurring species, and several hybrids. For the sub-tropical garden effect in cooler climates there are really only three species that have proven to overwinter successfully outside.

Musa basjoo has the ability to withstand several degrees of frost, although in cold sites it is worth mulching the roots and wrapping the main stems in hessian sacking. Cutting the leaves by half and slotting a plastic drain-pipe over the shoot, filling with straw and capping the top is another technique.

They are best grown in a sheltered site away from the wind, with regular liquid feeding in summer for ultimate growth. Large, globular green-yellow flowers may hang down on mature 2–3m (6–10ft) stems, often resulting in the stem dying off after the flowers have dropped.

Musa basjoo *at Bambouserie, Prafrance*

Musa sikkimensis likes similar conditions. The leaves are more variable with some forms having remarkable chocolate-red splashes and red-brown midribs. It makes a very striking and outstanding focal plant within the border.

Musa 'Yunnan' is new to cultivation, and collected from high altitudes in Yunnan, China. This plant may well prove to be quite cold-resilient in favoured locations, but it is still worth providing some winter protection.

Musa sikkimensis *growing in Abbotsbury Sub-tropical gardens*

Musella lasiocarpa

Family: Musaceae
Common name: Rock banana
Country of origin: China, Vietnam, Laos
Requirement: A position in full sun; needs frost protection in winter
USDA Zone: Z9

Musella resembles a dwarf *Ensete*, growing to about 1.2m (4ft) tall with luscious green foliage. It produces an unusual reddish-green pseudo-stem with a massive yellow flower head rather like a globe artichoke. It is new to Western cultivation and quite rare in the wild, yet is grown in China for pig food!

If your garden is not in a favourably mild area, winter protection will be needed, although it seems reasonably cold-tolerant. It will make a good container specimen for bringing in under glass for the winter.

Musella lasiocarpa

Strelitzia

Family: Strelitziaceae
Common name: Bird of paradise
Country of origin: South Africa
Requirement: A position in full sun and a moisture-retentive soil; needs frost protection in winter
USDA Zone: Z9

Strelitzia resembles *Musa* with its stout banana-like oblong, glaucous leaves. In the wilds of South Africa it grows in bold clumps, often found alongside riverbanks in deep rich soil. It is best known as a conservatory plant grown mainly for its exotic beaked bird of paradise flowers, yet it will grow outside in a sunny border for the summer, requiring plenty of organic matter to help keep the soil moist. When the weather gets cooler it should be lifted and containerized for the winter.

Strelitzia nicolai has the most tropical-looking leaves that can get to 2m (6ft) in ideal conditions. *Strelitzia reginae* is the true bird of paradise, with colourful flowers and slightly less robust foliage.

Strelitzia reginae

Strelitzia nicolai

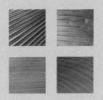

Grasses and bamboos
A-Z

When using large-foliage plants it is always a good idea to break up the overall design by planting an opposing leaf form and shape for added contrast. In Chinese culture Yin and Yang are the symbolic terms for the characteristics of opposing, yet complementary forces. In planting designs, this could perhaps be applied to upright forms being planted against horizontal; broad leaf against linear.

Large-leaved grasses and bamboos can be used for this effect, where they will add a sense of drama along with a touch of the tropics to any mixed exotic border. Selecting only the largest leaf forms has narrowed down the choice of species to ones that have a more sub-tropical effect.

Arundo donax

Family: Poaceae
Common name: Giant reed
Country of origin: Mediterranean
Requirement: A position in full sun or partial shade
USDA Zone: Z6

This is the largest and most tropical-looking grass for cool, temperate zones. The main stems can reach up to 5m (16ft) in warm regions and are self-supporting, with grey-green, coarse leaves, 7cm (3in) wide. In cold winters this grass will die back to the ground and send out enormous new shoots in the spring. It is not particular as to which soil to grow in, and can withstand periods of drought and even flooding. It forms tough, solid clumps which will propagate by dividing in the spring.

Arundo donax 'Variegata' is the striped giant reed, with pure white and green leaves in the spring, fading to yellow-green in hot summers. *Arundo donax* 'Macrophylla' is a form with broader and more glaucous leaves.

Arundo donax

Arundo donax *'Variegata'*

x Hibanobambusa tranquillans 'Shiroshima'

Family: Poaceae
Common name: None
Country of origin: Natural hybrid
Requirement: A position in full sun or partial shade
USDA Zone: Z7

This is one of the best of the variegated bamboos, having some of the largest evergreen leaves up to 25cm (10in) long and 5cm (2in) wide. It forms a dense bush up to 5m (16ft) which, although quite vigorous in growth, is not too difficult to keep under control.

The form 'Shiroshima' has clear cream-white striped leaves that make an outstanding backdrop in a sheltered semi-shady border.

x Hibanobambusa tranquillans *'Shiroshima'*

Indocalamus tessellatus

Family: Poaceae
Common name: None
Country of origin: China
Requirement: A position in full sun or partial shade; needs a moisture-retentive soil
USDA Zone: Z5

This small ground-covering bamboo has long spear-shaped, lanceolate, evergreen leaves up to 40cm (16in) long, forming distinctly tropical-looking culms to 3m (10ft) in height. It is slow-spreading, so not too invasive, unlike *Sasa* species with which this plant has often been confused. It was introduced from China into Britain in 1845, and grown for its tropical appearance (yet it is very hardy).

Indocalamus hamadae has probably the largest leaves of all the temperate bamboos, at up to 60cm (2ft) in length. Generally, this species does well in a moisture-retentive woodland soil with plenty of organic matter, in full sun or half-shade.

Indocalamus tessellatus

Miscanthus sacchariflorus x sinensis

Family: Poaceae
Common name: Giant miscanthus
Country of origin: Possible garden hybrid
Requirement: A place in full sun; a moisture-retentive soil is necessary
USDA Zone: Z4

This grass, which may still be found under its old name of *Miscanthus* x *giganteus*, is a wonderful clump-forming, upright grass growing up to 3m (10ft). It is suitable as a specimen plant on its own, or for the back of a border, or even as an ornamental hedge. The leaves are 2.5cm (1in) wide and cascade, making it an attractive and architectural feature.

The grass dies down at the end of the year and will need cutting back early to prevent winter gales blowing the dead leaf stems everywhere.

Miscanthus sacchariflorus *x* sinensis

Sasa

Family: Poaceae
Common name: None
Country of origin: Japan
Requirement: A position in full sun or partial shade
USDA Zone: Z5
Warning: Can be invasive

Although *Sasa* is classed as a dwarf bamboo, the larger species can develop into large-leaved, bold and jungle-like thickets. Take extreme caution when planting these on account of their invasive rhizomes. Where possible it is a good idea to plant these into 'root barriers' – tough, large, outer shelled growing sacks. Alternatively, they can be grown in large containers.

Sasa palmata nebulosa has brown markings on the older culms. *Sasa veitchii* is another strong ground cover plant for semi-shade, with distinct broad to ovate leaves that produce colour on the leaf margins in winter to create a white-parched edging that is very attractive. The form S. *veitchii minor* (sometimes seen as S. *veitchii nana*) has smaller leaves but more prominent markings.

Sasa palmata nebulosa

Sasa veitchii

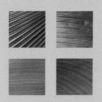

Bulbs, rhizomes and tubers A-Z

There are many fine bulbous plants that can be used successfully in the sub-tropical garden. Although chiefly grown for their flowering qualities, many actually combine flower colour with attractive, luscious foliage which will contribute to the overall jungle-like effect.

Alocasia

Family: Araceae
Common name: Elephants' ears, Taro
Country of origin: Tropical South and South-East Asia
Requirement: A position in partial shade, in moisture-retentive soil; needs frost protection in winter
USDA Zone: Z10

Alocasia is an edible, rhizomatous or tuberous perennial, with large evergreen or herbaceous leaves on erect stems. These luscious leaves are well named as elephants' ears, growing up to 1m (3ft) across.

This genus is truly tropical and there are over 70 species. In order to grow plants like these outside in a cool temperate garden one has to be realistic about the type of winter protection that can be provided. If in doubt then grow them in containers that can be put under cover for the winter.

Alocasia macrorrhiza produces large, veined, glossy leaves. It requires high humidity and a rich loam with well-rotted farmyard manure. It likes bright but indirect light. When winter temperatures drop below 15°C (59°F) it will lose its leaves, but it has been known to regrow in the spring after several degrees of frost, provided a thick layer of woodchip mulch has been applied. *Alocasia cucullata* is a species worth a try outside, requiring the same conditions.

Alocasia macrorrhiza

Amorphophallus konjac

Family: Araceae
Common name: Umbrella arum
Country of origin: South-East Asia
Requirement: A position in partial shade, in a moisture-retentive soil
USDA Zone: Z8

This unusual plant is grown from a corm. It produces a marbled dark-blotched petiole, supporting a magnificent compound leaf or spath, 55cm (22in) across, and looking rather like a blown out umbrella, hence its common name. It likes a shaded, moist spot with humus-rich soil.

The plant has a real tropical look and will grow quite happily under the canopy of taller shrubs or trees, which complements the exotic effect. It requires a mild garden with plenty of mulch for winter protection, or can be container grown and plunged outside for the summer.

Amorphophallus konjac

Arisaema costatum

Family: Araceae
Common name: None
Country of origin: Central and Eastern Nepal
Requirement: A position in part shade, in a moisture- retentive soil
USDA Zone: Z7

Forms of *Arisaema* are grown for their attractive, beautifully marked foliage and curiously hooded spathes. They are in the Aroid family, growing from a tuberous corm. In the wilds of Nepal these plants inhabit forest edges and road verges. In cultivation they are best grown in the semi-shade and shelter of a woodland garden, with plenty of leaf mould, and preferably a slightly acid loam soil.

Arisaema costatum has a very attractive purple-striped spathe on a white background, yet it is the magnificent leaf that dominates. It is dark green with a faint red edge, and comprises three sections, with the central leaflet getting to 30cm (12in) long and 15cm (6in) wide on a tall, stout petiole.

Canna

Family: Cannaceae
Common name: Canna lily
Country of origin: Tropical regions South America, Australia
Requirement: A position in full sun, in moisture-retentive soil; needs frost protection in winter
USDA Zone: Z9

Forms of *Canna* are famous for their exotic and brilliantly coloured flowers. They were favourite plants of the Victorians for summer bedding schemes, and they are still much used today in public parks the world over.

Canna indica

These are tender, rhizomatous perennial herbs, with thick fleshy roots. They will need either lifting, dividing and storing for the winter or, in reasonably mild gardens, they can be left out all winter, with a thick layer of mulch applied over the crown and roots, as long as they have adequate drainage. The large oval leaves can come in a vast range of colours and look stunning as a large drift or backdrop to a border or waterside feature. The Indian shot plant (*Canna indica*) may be slightly hardier than the hybrid cultivars. Its red and yellow flowers are smaller, and it produces an abundance of attractive globular seed heads, from which plenty of seed arises, which germinates readily.

Canna iridiflora makes a taller specimen with large leaves as much as 1.2m (4ft) long and 40cm (16in) wide, followed by nodding, rose-pink flowers.

Canna edulis is another tall stout-stemmed plant, up to 3m (10ft) high, with broad leaves and stems that are tinged purple. *Canna musifolia* is a real giant of a foliage plant, superb in big clumps, which can reach 2.5m (9ft) in height. With paddle-shaped leaves up to 60cm (2ft) long, it is often mistaken as a form of banana. Meanwhile, *Canna* 'Grande' is a real beauty with its gigantic foliage – huge, finely ribbed green leaves with dark red ribs and stem.

Canna iridiflora *'Ehemanii'*

Canna *'Durban'*

Canna musifolia

Colocasia esculenta

Family: Araceae
Common name: Imperial taro
Country of origin: Eastern Asia
Requirement: A position in partial shade, in moisture-retentive soil; needs frost protection in winter
USDA Zone: Z10

This is one of those plants that seems to defy the textbooks where cold sensitivity is concerned. It has been known to withstand several degrees of frost, and regrows from the tuber if it has been well mulched. But for those with a delicate disposition, or who garden in a really cold climate, then grow it in a container – just to be on the safe side. Plunge outside for the summer and lift the tuberous stems before winter sets in.

The leaves are robust and are particularly architectural, with their characteristic veins and marbled blue-black markings. They do especially well if grown in a sheltered moist site, such as at the edge of a stream. The typical aroid spathe is pale yellow.

In the humid lowland tropics they are grown as an important staple carbohydrate food, eaten boiled, baked or roasted.

Colocasia esculenta *'Illustris'*

Crinum x powellii

Family: Amaryllidaceae
Common name: None
Country of origin: Garden origin
Requirement: A position in full sun, in a moisture-retentive soil
USDA Zone: Z6

All *Crinum* are handsome bulbous plants that come from the warm and tropical regions of the world, yet there are one or two species that are suited to a sheltered temperate garden.

The garden hybrid *Crinum* x *powellii* is one of them. Its cultivars include 'Album' (pure white funnel-shaped flowers on tall stems), 'Roseum' (light pink), and 'Krelagei' (larger and dark pink). Apart from the flowers, the large strapping leaves, that are carried on elongated necks, are an impressive feature and grow to 1m (3ft) or longer.

They like a deep well-drained fertile soil that does not dry out too much. Give them a deep mulch protection and choose a site such as the base of a south-facing wall, to let them slowly establish. They resent transplanting, yet will produce offsets that can be divided.

Crinum x powellii *'Roseum'*

Curcuma zedoaria

Family: Zingiberaceae
Common name: Zedoary
Country of origin: India
Requirement: A position in partial shade; needs frost protection in winter
USDA Zone: Z10

This plant is a short-lived, rhizomatous perennial, with swollen aromatic roots that are used in the spice trade for a mild ginger pickle, and for their camphor-like perfumed oil. The leaf blades can be up to 80cm (32in) long, with an attractive deep purple midrib. It is a plant for glasshouse ground cover, or could be grown in large containers and plunged in the garden, given regular liquid feeding in summer, then taken in to dry off for winter dormancy under glass with a minimum temperature of 12°C (54°F).

Curcuma longa is the plant from which we get turmeric, the yellow dye and spice widely used in the tropics.

Curcuma zedoaria

Curcumorpha longiflora

Family: Zingiberaceae
Common name: None
Country of origin: North-East India, Himalayas
Requirement: A position in part shade; needs frost protection in winter
USDA Zone: Z9

Although little is known about this plant in a temperate climate, it certainly makes a fine cool greenhouse specimen with potential as a garden plant. It has elongated, *Hosta*-like, lime-green foliage, and produces attractive cream-white, red-tipped, short-flowering shoots that are almost hidden at the base of the leaves. It is likely to be a tricky plant in cultivation as it requires a period of intense moisture (provided in its natural habitat by monsoon rains), followed by a period of winter drought.

Curcumorpha longiflora

Dahlia imperialis

Family: Compositae
Common name: None
Country of origin: Mexico, Columbia, Guatemala
Requirement: A position in full sun; needs frost protection in winter
USDA Zone: Z9

Unlike the decorative garden hybrid *Dahlia*, this species is a giant sub-shrub, reaching 9m (30ft) in a hot, sunny climate. The woody stems have large 60cm (2ft) long pinnate leaves crowned with nodding pale lilac to white flowers. In cool temperate climates it rarely reaches these proportions.

It can be grown in containers and brought into growth under glass, then transferred to the garden for the summer. Keep it well watered, and liquid feed during the growing season.

Dahlia imperialis

Dracunculus vulgaris

Family: Araceae
Common name: Dragon arum
Country of origin: Central and East Mediterranean
Requirement: A position in full sun or part shade
USDA Zone: Z9

The dragon arum is an unusual tuberous herbaceous perennial. It produces basal leaves around a large mottled sheath that forms a pseudo-stem. From this emerges a large black-red spathe, looking like tropical foliage. But beware, it smells of rotting carcass in order to attract flies for pollination.

Dracunculus vulgaris requires deep, moist and well-drained soil in order to grow well, ideally followed by a period of summer drought for the tuber to go dormant. It will tolerate several degrees of frost, but it is certainly a good idea to mulch with bracken or well-rotted manure before winter sets in.

Dracunculus vulgaris

Eucomis

Family: Liliaceae
Common name: Pineapple lily
Country of origin: South Africa
Requirement: A position in full sun
USDA Zone: Z8

These are large, perennial bulbous plants with a basal rosette of broad glossy leaves and star-shaped green flowers on long stems in late summer. *Eucomis bicolor* has oblong leaves 40cm (16in) long and 10cm (4in) wide, and cylindrical, maroon-flecked flower heads resembling small pineapples. *Eucomis* 'Zeal Bronze' has straplike purple-green leaves up to 60cm (2ft) long. *Eucomis pole-evansii* has even larger leaves at 1.1m (3¹/₂ft) long and 15cm (6in) wide.

They are all suitable for a warm sunny site in well-drained soil. Cover the crowns with a protective mulch in winter, or grow in containers and keep under glass. They can be propagated from offsets or spring-sown seed.

Eucomis bicolor

Eucomis *'Zeal Bronze'*

Hedychium

Family: Zingiberaceae
Common name: Ginger lilies
Country of origin: China, India, Himalayas
Requirement: A position in full sun or part shade, in a moisture-retentive soil
USDA Zone: Z9

Hedychiums are grown for their showy scented flowers that appear in late summer. Although very beautiful the individual flowers do not last long, yet the large and glossy leaves are present from early summer onwards, forming the perfect exotic foliage clump. These are rhizomatous perennials suited to leafy soil that is moist in summer for good growth, followed by a dry and frost-free winter. Many are true tropical species requiring a winter minimum of 18°C (66°F).

Hedychium gardnerianum is one of the toughest and will take some frost as long as the main crown is well mulched. *Hedychium forrestii* makes a good forest edge subject, with robust dark green leaves and pure white, lightly scented flowers.

Hedychium greenei has wonderful glossy leaves, dark green above and maroon beneath, up to 25cm (10in) long, followed by large cone-shaped red to orange flower spikes. Others worth trying in a well-protected site, such as at the base of a south-facing wall, are *Hedychium coccinium, H. densiflorum* and *H. spicatum*.

They reproduce by small bulbil offsets.

Hedychium forrestii

Hedychium gardnerianum

Phytolacca

Family: Phytolaccaceae
Common name: Pokeweed
Country of origin: America, Mexico, China
Requirement: A position in full sun or part shade
USDA Zone: Z4/Z10

Some forms of *Phytolacca* can endure Zone 4, whilst others are happier in Zone 10. It is somewhat of a variable genus where preferred temperatures are concerned.

Phytolacca americana is a shrubby herbaceous species with ovate to elliptic, deciduous leaves up to 30cm (12in) long. They produce attractive, poisonous, red to purple berries that look particularly good in the autumn. These are spread by birds which can make the plant become an invasive weed if not controlled. They suit woodland planting in moisture-retentive soil.

Phytolacca dioica is a much larger evergreen, treelike species, producing quite a large trunk and broad crown. It comes from South America and grows in Zone 9, so requires a warm and sheltered site.

Phytolacca americana

Rhodea japonica

Family: Liliaceae
Common name: None
Country of origin: South-Western China, Japan
Requirement: A position in part shade, in a moisture-retentive soil
USDA Zone: Z7

This is a little known rhizomatous perennial with thick basal rosettes of spear-shaped, dark glossy green leaves, up to 45cm (18in) long and 7cm (3in) wide. It produces a fleshy white-yellow, short-flowering spike. Red or yellow berries come later.

This plant is suited to woodland conditions with part shade, in a humus-rich soil with plenty of leaf mould and moisture. When planted in a large group, it makes an excellent shade-loving ground cover, possessing a real jungle-like appearance.

Rhodea japonica

Xanthosoma violaceum

Family: Araceae
Common name: Blue taro
Country of origin: West Indies
Requirement: A position in full sun, in a moisture-retentive soil
USDA Zone: Z10

In the tropics the taro produces tubers or cormels, which are an important source of edible carbohydrate. They are grown in temperate gardens for their stunning ornamental foliage. The individual green leaves can grow to 70cm (28in) long and 45cm (18in) wide, with triangular basal lobes. The veins and midrib are purple, on long stalks.

This plant requires a mild, damp spot in a sheltered garden, in which the winter minimum stays above freezing. Alternatively, it will grow in a container that is kept well watered in summer, then brought in under glass when the temperatures drop.

Xanthosoma violaceum *at Bambouserie, Prafrance*

Zantedeschia aethiopica

Family: Araceae
Common name: Calla lily, arum lily
Country of origin: South Africa
Requirement: A position in full sun or part shade, in a moisture-retentive soil
USDA Zone: Z8

Well known by florists for its magnificent white blooms, the arum lily also makes a handsome foliage plant. The leaves can get to 1.2m (4ft) in length, are oblong to triangular, and sometimes have green-white translucent spots.

Occurring in the wild in wetland areas, these are adaptable plants. They can be grown as strong focal clumps in a cool moist border, as container specimens, or bog garden or marginal pond plants.

Generally *Zantedeschia* can take temperatures to -5°C (23°F) for short periods of time, helped with a thick organic mulch over the crown as it dies down for winter. However, Z. *aethiopica* is the hardiest form, tolerating low temperatures of some -10°C (14°F).

The form 'Crowborough' is pure white, and 'Green Goddess' has a large spathe with a green and white centre.

Zantedeschia aethiopica 'Crowborough' at the Royal Horticultural Society's garden at Wisley, Surrey, England

Moisture-loving and waterside plants A-Z

Anyone creating an exotic feel to their garden in a temperate climate will have a challenge on their hands. Diversity is the key to being successful with plants.

If it is possible to create a damp area, or use the natural features available to grow moisture-loving – or bog garden – plants, the choice of large-leaved species increases, along with the capabilities of making the 'cool tropics' really work with hardy plants.

Darmera peltata

Family: Saxifragaceae
Common name: Umbrella plant, Indian rhubarb
Country of origin: Western United States
Requirement: A position in partial shade, in a moisture-retentive soil
USDA Zone: Z6

This is a plant for damp streamside conditions, with deciduous peltate leaves up to 60cm (2ft) across, emerging from a dense mat of creeping rhizome. It is a hardy plant from the mountains of the Californian Sierra Nevada, where it colonizes streamsides and muddy banks.

It likes wet but well-drained, humus-rich soil. In the spring the rounded, pink flower heads appear on tall stems before the emergence of the dramatic foliage. The plant is not a true exotic in that sense, but can imitate the tropics with its large bold leaves that mimic the jungle floor. Remember that its deciduous qualities will leave the area it occupies devoid of foliage in winter.

Darmera peltata

Gunnera manicata

Family: Haloragidaceae
Common name: Giant rhubarb
Country of origin: Brazil, Chile
Requirement: A position in full sun, in a moisture-retentive soil
USDA Zone: Z8

Gunnera manicata is an architectural perennial with gigantic leaves up to 3m (10ft) across, formed on prickly petioles that hold the huge leaves upwards like a parasol. It makes a magnificent waterside subject, or can be grown in border soil that is moisture-retentive, perhaps with the aid of a butyl liner dug into the soil. It is a good idea to fold the leaves over the crown for winter protection when they start to collapse at the end of the year, or to cover the crown with an organic mulch.

Gunnera tinctoria comes from Chile and will grow in a drier situation. It is a slightly smaller species, still with enormous leaves however, and needs similar winter protection.

Gunnera manicata

Lysichiton americanus

Family: Araceae
Common name: Skunk cabbage
Country of origin: California to Alaska
Requirement: A position in full sun or partial shade, in a moisture-retentive soil
USDA Zone: Z6

This is a plant well suited to swamps, wet woodland or the bog garden, with lots of deep humus-rich soil. It is primarily grown for its early spring inflorescences of a white sheath with bright yellow spathe. Its lush, bold, bright green leaves can have a jungle floor appearance and would blend in quite well with other more exotic species.

Do not be put off by its other less favourable quality of putting out a musky odour from the leaves, hence its common name.

Lysichiton americanus

Nelumbo nucifera

Family: Nelumbonaceae
Common name: Sacred lotus flower
Country of origin: Asia, Japan, Australia
Requirement: A position in full sun, in moistur-retentive soil; needs frost protection in winter
USDA Zone: Z9

The sacred lotus is one of the most beautiful large-leaved waterlilies. Leaves can reach 1m (3ft) across, and are lifted high above the water on tall stems. Flowers are pink to white, and scented. The best way to grow it in temperate gardens is in a watertight woodenhalf-barrel, kept in the greenhouse until temperatures have warmed up outside. Then move it to a warm, sunny, sheltered patio. It will need storing in a frost-free place over winter.

Nelumbo nucifera

Thalia dealbata

Family: Marantaceae
Common name: None
Country of origin: Southern United States, Mexico
Requirement: A position in full sun or partial shade, and in moisture-retentive soil; requires frost protection in winter
USDA Zone: Z9

These are handsome plants, suitable for open sites in sub-tropical gardens. They perform best in a rich loam compost in shallow water or wet soil. Their grey-green foliage and graceful, tall inflorescences can make a real impact when planted en masse at the side of a pond for bold effect. In cool temperate gardens they can withstand a winter minimum temperature of -7°C (19°F), as long as the roots are 60cm (2ft) below the water level.

They also produce decorative tubular spikes of violet flowers, followed by attractive seed-heads. Remove any fading foliage during the growing season, to keep that fresh look.

Thalia dealbata

Garden succulents A-Z

One of the most exciting plants that you are likely to encounter on any holiday to a warm Mediterranean or tropical climate would be the century plant (*Agave*). These are giant succulents, with rosettes of large, fleshy, rigid, spine-tipped leaves. They are more often regarded as a house plant in temperate gardens, as many turn to pulp as soon as they are frosted. Yet, surprisingly, there are some species that can withstand quite severe cold as long as certain growing conditions are provided.

There are many other handsome evergreen plants with spiky profiles that can also be grown, all having strong architectural qualities that are so important for the structure and make-up of the sub-tropical landscape. Here is a selection of plants with the broadest leaf forms; most have proven to survive outside in some of the more favourable parts of the UK.

Aeonium

Family: Crassulaceae
Common name: None
Country of origin: Canary Islands, Madeira, Yemen, East Africa
Requirement: A position in full sun; good plant for coastal gardens; needs frost protection in winter
USDA Zone: Z9

The *Aeonium* is a succulent perennial or small shrub with soft fleshy leaf rosettes. It is well suited to being grown in the cool greenhouse or as a specimen in a pot, and this practice is certainly best for really cold sites. However, if you have a south-facing slope within a mild garden where the cold air would run away, then experiment with some permanent planting.

They will need a gritty, free-draining soil that does not dry out too much. In winter, small cloches can be placed over the tops to keep the worst of the driving rain off, but in freezing conditions they will need a thick layer of insulation material packed in around the stems.

Aeonium canariense can produce enormous dinner plate size rosettes up to 40cm (16in) across. *Aeonium arboreum* 'Atropurpureum' has fleshy leaves that are smaller and dark garnet in colour. They are tender and not the easiest to overwinter outside as cold rains can make them rot easily. *Aeonium cuneatum* makes an attractive subject on a sloping bank as it spreads and carpets with stoloniferous shoots.

Aeonium arboreum *'Atropurpureum'*

Aeonium canariense

Aeonium cuneatum *taken at Lamorran House, St Mawes, Cornwall, England*

Agave

Family: Agavaceae
Common name: Century plant
Country of origin: North America, Mexico
Requirement: A position in full sun or partial shade; needs frost protection in winter
USDA Zone: Z9

Plants in this genus have, in general, large fleshy leaves in a spiral rosette. This is a desert adaptation that encourages water droplets to run centrally down to the root zone. They are often monocarpic, flowering once in their lifetime and then dieing. For general growing conditions in cooler temperate gardens they need acute drainage at the roots, preferably on a free-draining slope, and with a clean gravel mulch around the basal leaves to keep surface water away. Mini-tunnels or cloches over the plants in winter also help keep driving rain off.

Agave americana

Agaves will grow well in pots, even when they are 'pot bound' or root crowded, and make excellent subjects for courtyards or patios, with only occasional light feeding and watering needed during the hottest spells.

They produce offsets or 'pups' that are easy enough to cut away from the parent plant and grow on.

There are over 580 species of *Agave*, with many yet to be tried and tested in cooler climates. It is surprising that so many desert plants can take really cold conditions: *A. chrysantha*, *A. palmeri* and *A. celsii* have been recorded to survive -10°C (14°F), and even tougher are *A. parryi*, *A. utahensis* and *A.harvardiana*, which have been known to survive as low as -18°C (0°F).

Agave celsii *on Herm, Channel Islands*

Agave utahensis

Agave americana *'Variegata'*

Aloe

Family: Liliaceae
Common name: Aloe, Torch plant
Country of origin: South Africa, Tropical Africa, Madagascar
Requirement: A position in full sun; needs frost protection in winter
USDA Zone: Z9

These are plants mostly suited to arid and semi-arid climates, or grown as important succulent collections under glass. It is a diverse family of plants ranging from perennial herbs to shrubs with well-developed trunks. For growing outside all year round in cooler climates the choice is limited; it is better to keep them in containers and plunge them in the garden for the summer.

Although not the largest-leaved species, *Aloe striatula* does seem to be one of the hardiest, experiencing -5°C (23°F) with no damage. The shrublike succulent *Aloe arborescens* has grey-green fleshy leaves up to 60cm (2ft) in length. It is not quite so tough, but worth trying in a sheltered spot in full sun, preferably with good drainage. *Aloe plicatilis* makes a grand multi-branched, treelike specimen in the rocky wilds of South Africa, with stiff, flattened, fleshy and architectural leaves.

Others that can take a couple of degrees of frost, are A. *africana*, A. *ferox*, A. *tenuir* and A. *marlothii*. They may well be worth trying outside if you have a good microclimate. All forms of *Aloe* tolerate poor, low fertile soils, are drought-resistant, and propagate easily from seed or stem cuttings.

Aloe arborescens

Aloe striatula

Aloe plicatilis

Beschorneria yuccoides

Family: Agavaceae
Common name: None
Country of origin: Mexico
Requirement: A position in full sun; good plant for coastal gardens
USDA Zone: Z9

These are evergreen perennials producing rosettes of large fleshy, glaucous, lance-shaped leaves, to 1.2m (4ft) long and 7.5cm (3in) wide. They are related to the *Agave*. The flower is a tall, showy, arching inflorescence, with pinkish-red bracts.

Given a sheltered position in a generally mild garden they are easily grown. Being quite drought-resistant, they make a great feature on a sunny sloping bank.

Beschorneria yuccoides

Doryanthes

Family: Agavaceae
Common name: Spear lily
Country of origin: Eastern Australia
Requirement: A position in full sun; needs frost protection in winter
USDA Zone: Z10

A large, handsome, clump-forming perennial, with fleshy, upright, sword-shaped leaves. The tall flower spikes consist of dense panicles of small orange and red bracts. They can make excellent stately specimens on their own, or grouped in a border or lawn. Best grown in a warm or maritime garden that is frost-free. Propagate from seed or from the mature bulbils.

Doryanthes palmeri *(Photo courtesy: Ian Watt)*

Furcraea

Family: Agavaceae
Common name: None
Country of origin: Mexico, Central America
Requirement: A position in full sun or partial shade; needs frost protection in winter
USDA Zone: Z9

This plant is another close relative of *Agave*, with attractive sword-shaped foliage in dense rosettes. Grow in full sun to half-shade, in a fertile soil with good drainage. It can take a light frost if kept dry at the root zone in winter, otherwise a mild maritime location is favourable.

Furcraea longaeva makes a large, ornamental, firmly structured plant, producing an enormous 10m (33ft) inflorescence in a candelabra shape.

The individual flowers are pale white, and droop down. These eventually form small bulbils which drop off and root themselves. The main rosette then dies after flowering.

Furcraea selloa var *marginata* has cream-yellow stripes along the leaf margins. It is well suited to container growing in cooler temperate conditions where it will be necessary to keep it under cover in winter.

Furcraea selloa *var* marginata

Furcraea longaeva

Puya chilensis

Family: Bromeliaceae
Common name: Bromeliad
Country of origin: Chile
Requirement: A position in full sun; needs frost protection in winter
USDA Zone: Z8

This is one of the largest of the terrestrial bromeliads, growing on the high, arid hillsides of central Chile. It has a wonderfully exotic appearance with a dense rosette of viciously hooked spines along the straight, pale green 1m (3ft) long leaves.

Its flowers are formed on tall erect spikes, with yellow-green petals and bright yellow anthers. It is a plant for mild, sheltered areas although it can take several degrees of frost for short periods. In winter, small mini-tunnels or cloches can be placed over the plant to keep it dry and frost-free.

Puya chilensis

Yucca

Family: Agavaceae
Common name: None
Country of origin: North America, Mexico
Requirement: A position in full sun; good plant for coastal gardens
USDA Zone: Z4/Z10

Yuccas are grown for their outstanding ornamental sculptural leaf form.

As focal points within a courtyard garden, they really add a touch of drama with their exotic appearance. Many are totally hardy and they range in habit from bold, ground-hugging rosettes, to tall-stemmed treelike forms.

Well suited to sunny seaside gardens, they like good drainage and shelter from cold drying winds. *Yucca recurvifolia, Y. gloriosa* and

Y. filamentosa are cold-tolerant to about Z7 – around -15°C (5°F). Other more tender species such as *Y. elephantipes* (more often regarded as the house plant yucca) can be grown outside in cool temperate gardens provided adequate shelter and good drainage are provided.

Yucca aloifolia is known as Spanish bayonet, or the dagger plant, because of its stiff leaves with razor-sharp needles on the tips. One important tip: avoid planting it too close to a pathway because those leaves do bite!

Yucca elephantipes

Yucca aloifolia *'Marginata'*

Yucca recurvifolia *var* marginata *at Rosemoor Gardens, Devon, England*

Yucca gloriosa *'Variegata'*

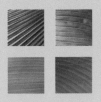

Annuals A-Z

Annuals can often be overlooked when designing and creating the sub-tropical style garden, especially when there are so many more permanent architectural plants available. By definition, annuals are plants that complete their entire life cycle in one year's growing season. In the UK we grow many tender plants as annuals (that die at the end of the year when the first frosts come), yet in their native countries where there are far warmer climates, they would be classed as perennials.

Annuals can be good border infillers, whilst waiting for other plants to become established. The choice is somewhat limited when it comes to large-leaved species, as annuals are generally grown for flowers and colour impact.

Amaranthus tricolor

Family: Amaranthaceae
Common name: Tampala
Country of origin: Africa, China
Requirement: A position in full sun
USDA Zone: Z10

This annual is invaluable for sub-tropical bedding schemes, especially as it comes in a range of garden varieties, all with stunning leaf colour. Reds, maroons and oranges are the main colours. On top of their foliage they produce quite attractive tassel plume flowers.

The leaves can be up to 23cm (9in) long and 10cm (4in) wide, ovate to elliptic, on long 8cm (3$\frac{1}{2}$in) petioles. The form 'Joseph's Coat' has a more erect habit with leaves scarlet, crimson and gold, whilst 'Illumination' has bright rose-red upper leaves, crimson and bronze beneath.

Amaranthus tricolor *(Photo courtesy: Graham Clarke)*

Nicotiana

Family: Solanaceae
Common name: Tobacco
Country of origin: Tropical America, Australia
Requirement: A position in full sun or partial shade
USDA Zone: Z8

These plants are mainly grown for their ornamental perfumed flowers, yet there are larger-leaved species that make handsome summer plantings in the border.

Nicotiana tobacum, the true tobacco plant, can have luscious, ovate to elliptic leaves up to 25cm (10in) long and can look most impressive when grown in a large group.

Nicotiana tobacum var *macrophylla* is an annual (or biennial) with even larger undulate, cordate leaves, to 40cm (16in), followed by rose-red flowers. *Nicotiana sylvestris* makes a robust plant up to 1.5m (5ft) in height. It has ascending, elliptic leaves, sticky to touch, up to 30cm (12in) long, with white, pendant and scented flowers. This species sometimes overwinters like a perennial in sheltered, mild gardens, but the vigour is lost in the second year, so growing from seed each year produces a stronger plant. All Nicotiana are poisonous as they contain the alkaloid nicotine.

Nicotiana sylvestris *(Photo courtesy: Graham Clarke)*

Ricinus communis

Family: Euphorbiaceae
Common name: Castor oil plant
Country of origin: South-East Mediterranean, North-East Africa
Requirement: A position in full sun; needs a moisture-retentive soil
USDA Zone: Z10
Warning: Produces poisonous seeds

This is a magnificent bold foliage plant, traditionally grown as an annual dot plant amongst sub-tropical bedding, or as a pot plant specimen for the conservatory. The leaves are up to 60cm (2ft) long, purplish and palmately lobed, followed by conspicuous spiny fruit, which contain the deadly poisonous substance ricin. Take care when planting in areas where the seed can ripen and where children can access the plants.

There are various cultivars available, such as 'Gibsonii', dwarf to 1.2m (4ft), with black-purple stems and a purple metallic sheen to the leaves. 'Zanzibariensis' has very large green leaves with white veins. 'Impala' produces carmine young growth followed by clusters of sulphur-yellow flowers.

Ricinus communis

Ricinus communis

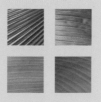

Climbers A-Z

Gardeners creating the exotic look in a cool climate will find it a challenge selecting suitably impressive large-leaved climbers that instil that exotic flavour or mimic jungle creepers and vines. The giant climbing vine-like Swiss cheese plant (*Monstera deliciosa*) with its luscious leaves would be just the right kind of plant – if it didn't need hot and humid 'tropical' conditions.

However, with careful selection there are several attractive climbing plants that can be used in the cool exotic-style garden that would not look out of place alongside more tropical partners. The following selection comprises climbers I have successfully grown outside in the sheltered maritime climate of England's south coast.

Actinidia deliciosa

Family: Actinidiaceae
Common name: Kiwi fruit, Chinese gooseberry
Country of origin: China
Requirement: A position in full sun or partial shade
USDA Zone: Z7

Best known as the commercial kiwi fruit, this climber actually makes a very attractive foliage plant, with large 20cm (8in) wide leaves on downy-red shoots that can twine their way up through old trees or cover a wall. They succeed in part shade, but if you want the added bonus of fruit you will need both male and female plants for successful pollination, together with full sun and shelter.

Actinidia deliciosa

Aristolochia macrophylla

Family: Aristolochiaceae
Common name: Dutchman's pipe
Country of origin: Eastern United States
Requirement: A position in full sun or partial shade
USDA Zone: Z6

This is a vigorous twining plant useful for covering old walls or scrambling through trees. It is deciduous, with large heart-shaped leaves up to 30cm (12in) long, and with tubular, yellowish-green, pitcher-shaped flowers. It will grow in sun or shade in most fertile soils but it is prone to snail and slug damage in the spring.

Aristolochia macrophylla

Clematis armandii

Family: Ranunculaceae
Common name: Clematis
Country of origin: Central and Western China
Requirement: A position in full sun; needs a moisture-retentive soil
USDA Zone: Z8

This is one of the best strong-growing, evergreen climbers. It can reach up to 6m (20ft), and is best grown on a warm sheltered wall, although it seems to take some shade as well. The leathery leaves are a dark glossy green, and grouped in three, each leaflet up to 10–20cm (4–8in) long. The cream-white flowers are carried in auxiliary clusters in mid-spring. The cultivar 'Snowdrift' has pure white flowers, and 'Apple Blossom' has white to dappled-pink sepals.

Clematis armandii

Cucurbita

Family: Cucurbitaceae
Common name: Gourd
Country of origin: Tropical America
Requirement: A position in full sun or partial shade; needs frost protection in winter
USDA Zone: Z10

This is the plant family that contains ornamental gourds, edible marrows, pumpkins and squashes. I have tried growing them in the mixed border where they can weave their way through, up and over other plants in a jungle-like manner. When grown as an annual they can make quite an impact in one summer with their enormous leaves up to 30cm (12in) long.

Grow them in well-drained soils with plenty of organic matter. Fruits are a bonus but you can pinch out any flowers to concentrate on the foliage. *Cucurbita pepo* and C. *moschata* both have colourful red, green, white and yellow gourds. *Cucurbita ficifolia* is likely to be one of the most hardy forms, often grown as a perennial in warmer climates.

An archway of Cucurbita leaves

x Fatshedera lizei

Family: Araliaceae
Common name: Fat-headed Lizzie
Country of origin: Garden hybrid (France, 1910)
Requirement: A position in full sun or partial shade
USDA Zone: Z7

An attractive evergreen shrub with stout shoots that semi-climb, but require some support on fences, trees or posts.

One of the parents of this hybrid plant is a form of the glossy-leaved paper plant (*Fatsia japonica* 'Moseri') and the other is an ivy (*Hedera hibernica*) so there is some resemblance to both species in its large glossy leaves. Cultivars include 'Annemieke' with yellow variegated leaves, and 'Pia' with undulated wavy leaf edges.

x Fatshedera lizei *'Variegata'*

Hedera

Family: Araliaceae
Common name: Ivy
Country of origin: Canary Islands, Azores, Europe, Caucasus, Southern Asia
Requirement: A position in full sun or partial shade
USDA Zone: Z5/Z8

The ivies need no introduction. They are hardy, evergreen climbers that thrive in most soils and situations, either in sun or full shade, and they even tolerate atmospheric pollution well.

The larger-leaved forms can have a place in the sub-tropical garden as they cling by aerial roots and are jungle-like in habit.

The Persian ivy (*Hedera colchica* 'Dentata Variegata') has very large leaves that are conspicuously margined creamy yellow to creamy white. *Hedera colchica* 'Sulphur Heart' has a boldly marked central splash of yellow.

The Canary Island ivy (*H. canariensis* 'Gloire de Marengo') has glossy bright green leaves in the centre, merging to silver grey with cream-white margins.

Hedera canariensis *'Gloire de Marengo'*

Humulus lupulus 'Aureus'

Family: Cannabaceae
Common name: Common hop
Country of origin: Temperate Europe, Central Asia, North America
Requirement: A position in full sun
USDA Zone: Z5

This rapid-growing herbaceous climber will happily scramble up and through trellis or over a tree. The form 'Aureus' has striking golden, lobed and coarsely toothed leaves that colour up well especially if planted in full sun.

It is well known for producing blossom known as 'hops', used for brewing beer. The whole plant dies down at the end of the year, which can leave a bare gap on your trellis until regrowth occurs in the spring. They are hardy down to -15°C (5°F).

Humulus lupulus *'Aureus'*

Lonicera hildebrandiana

Family: Caprifoliaceae
Common name: Giant honeysuckle
Country of origin: South-East Asia, China
Requirement: A position in full sun; needs frost protection in winter
USDA Zone: Z9

The giant honeysuckle is a real gem of a plant. It has rampant growth with semi-evergreen glossy green leathery leaves, up to 15cm (6in) long. The sweetly scented flowers are beautiful, with long tubular petals, cream-white turning rich orange. It requires a sheltered, almost frost-free environment with full sun.

Lonicera hildebrandiana

Luffa cylindrical

Family: Cucurbitaceae
Common name: Loofah
Country of origin: Africa, Asia
Requirement: A position in full sun or partial shade; needs frost protection in winter
USDA Zone: Z9

Grown throughout the tropics for its edible fruits and large yellow flowers. The dried vascular inner parts of the fruits are where loofah sponges come from. These are annuals that rapidly spread and cover any trellis with their palmate and three-lobed leaves up to 20cm (8in) across, held up by climbing tendrils. In our cooler summers they may need some tender loving care, first under glass to get them established before planting out.

Passiflora

Family: Passifloraceae
Common name: Passion flower
Country of origin: Asia, New Zealand, Australia, Central and South America
Requirement: A position in full sun; needs frost protection in winter
USDA Zone: Z9

Passion flowers, with their exotic flowers and vigorous climbing stems, are a true symbol of tropical and sub-tropical climates. They are mostly species for sheltered, warm and humid gardens, with only a few hardy species such as *P. caerulea*, *P. lutea* and *P. incarnata* being suitable for temperate areas.

Large-leaved forms are mostly tropical, but *P. alata* may be worth trying outside in a very mild garden. It has ovate leaves up to 15cm (6in) long, and bears fragrant crimson flowers and edible fruits. It can take -1°C (30°F) for short periods and may be best grown as a container plant outside for the summer, or as a conservatory subject.

Passiflora alata

Vitis

Family: Vitaceae
Common name: Vine
Country of origin: Japan, China, North America
Requirement: A position in full sun or partial shade
USDA Zone: Z5

Ornamental vines can be grown for their luxuriant foliage, rapid growth and superb autumn colour. The biggest-leaved varieties can add a touch of jungle-like quality if allowed to wander in a controlled fashion.

Vitis coignetiae can rapidly cover a tree, and turns a deep scarlet in the autumn. *Vitis amurensis* is another strong-growing deciduous climber with leaves to 25cm (10in) long.

For best colouring, grow all of these in moisture-retentive soil and a warm site. They will also grow well in partial shade.

Vitis coignetiae

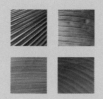

Botanical glossary

The following is a list of botanical terms used in this book for describing leaf form and shape, or plant definition:

Compound Divided into two or more parts

Cordate Heart-shaped

Corm Swollen, subterranean, bulb-like stem

Cormel Small corm developing from around the main or parent corm

Corolla Whorl of petals in a flower

Elliptic Regularly rounded, between oblong and ovate, with narrowed ends

Entire Margins uninterrupted, not toothed or lobed

Fronds Large compound leaf, as demonstrated by such plants as palms and ferns

Glaucous Coated with a fine whitish blue-green film

Globular Composed of near spherical shape

Inflorescence The arrangement of flowers and all their components on a stem

Irregular-toothed The shape being asymmetrical

Juvenile Non-adult phases of a plant's life where juvenile foliage may differ

Lanceolate 3–6 times long as broad; lance-shaped

Linear Slender and elongated

Lobed Divided into segments, separated from adjacent segments (as with 'fingers')

Marginate Conspicuous margin or border

Maritime Confined to the coastal area

Midrib Primary vein of a leaf or leaflet, running down its centre

Oblong 2-3 times long as broad, usually possessing parallel sides

Ovate Rounded at both ends, broadest in the middle; egg-shaped

Palmate Three or more lobes or segments, palm-like, from same basal point

Peltate Stalk is attached inside at the margin rather than at the edge

Petiole Leaf stalk

Pitcher-shaped Tubular cuplike vessel from a modified leaf tip

Pinnate An arrangement of leaflets in two rows; feather-like

Pseudo False or apparently, but not actually; used as a prefix as in pseudo-bulb or pseudo-stem

Raceme An unbranched inflorescence with many small-stalked flowers

Ray florets A small flower with a tubular corolla

Rhizome Swollen, specialized stem, subterranean or close to soil surface

Sagittate Arrow or spear-shaped; triangular basal lobes

Spadix The finger-like centre of a spathe

Spathe A conspicuous bract or leaf subtending a spadix or inflorescence

Terminal The extreme tip or apex of a stem, the summit of an axis

Trilobed Having three lobes

Tomentum Pubescence, fine hairs

Tuber Swollen branch or root, generally subterranean

Umbel Flat-topped inflorescence with all flowered rays arising from same point

Vascular Tissues or vessels that conduct water

Xerophyte Plant that has adapted to survival in arid conditions

Recommended reading

Any of the following books make good reading for anyone looking for useful information on growing plants with an exotic 'feel':

The New Exotic Garden by Will Giles
ISBN 1840002417

The Subtropical Garden by Gil Hanly & Jacqueline Walker ISBN 08811923591

Hot Plants for Cool Climates
by S. Roth & D. Schrader ISBN 0395963230

Bananas you can Grow
by James Waddick & Glenn Stokes ISBN 0967854016

The Palm Identifier by Martin Gibbons
ISBN 1850764069

Palms Throughout the World by David L. Jones
ISBN 0730104206

Encyclopaedia of Ferns by David L. Jones
ISBN 0881920541

Tropical Garden Style with Hardy Plants
by Alan Hemsley ISBN 1861082371

Tender Perennials by Ian Cooke ISBN 0715306359

The Gardeners' Guide to Growing Cannas
by Ian Cooke ISBN 071531131

Agaves, Yuccas and Related Plants
by Mary & Gary Irish ISBN 0881924423

Exotic Gardening in Cool Climates
by Myles Challis ISBN 1857021878

The Gardeners' Guide to Growing Temperate Bamboos by Michael Bell ISBN 0715308599

Hardy Palms and Palm-like Plants
by Martyn Graham ISBN 1 86108 267 3

A Beginners' Guide to Water Gardening
by Graham Clarke ISBN 1861082436

Exotics Are Easy (compilation of articles)
ISBN 1861082312

Gardens to visit

These cool temperate gardens are open to the public, and they are known for growing exotic-looking plants with architectural bold foliage:

British Isles

Abbotsbury Sub-tropical Gardens, Abbotsbury, Weymouth, Dorset

Bristol Zoo, Clifton, Bristol

Chelsea Physic Garden, 66 Royal Hospital Road, London

Chester Zoo, Chester, Cheshire

Coleton Fishacre, Kingswear, Dartmouth, Devon (National Trust)

Chumleigh Gardens, Chumleigh, Burgess Park, London

Cotswold Wildlife Park, Burford, Oxfordshire

Dunster Castle, Dunster, Minehead, Somerset

Eden Project, Bodelva, St Austell, Cornwall

Glendurgan, Mawnan Smith, Falmouth, Cornwall (National Trust)

Great Dixter, Northiam, Hastings, Sussex

Heligan Gardens, Pentwan, St Austell, Cornwall

Inverewe, Poolewe, NW Highlands (National Trust for Scotland)

Lamorran, Upper Castle Road, St Mawes, Truro, Cornwall

Logan Botanical Garden, Port Logan, Stranraer, Scotland

Mount Stewart, Newtownards, Co. Down (National Trust)

Overbecks, Sharpitor, Salcombe, Devon (National Trust)

Paignton Zoo, Totnes Road, Paignton, Devon

Penjerrick Gardens, Mawnan Smith, Falmouth, Cornwall

Pine Lodge Gardens, Cuddra, St Austell, Cornwall

Portmerrion, Penrhyndeudraeth, Gwynedd, North Wales

Powys Castle, Welshpool, Powys

Royal Botanical Gardens, Kew, Richmond, London

Royal Horticultural Society Gardens, Wisley and Rosemoor

Torosay Castle, Caignure, Isle of Mull, Argyll

Trebah, Mawnan Smith, Falmouth, Cornwall

Tregrehan, Par, Cornwall

Trelissick, Feock, Truro, Cornwall

Trenwainton, Madron, Penzance, Cornwall (National Trust)

Tresco Abbey Gardens, Tresco, Isles of Scilly, Cornwall

The Old Vicarage, East Runton, Norfolk

The Exotic Garden, 6 Cotman Road, Thorpe, Norwich (open by arrangement)

Ventnor Botanical Gardens, Steephill Road, Ventnor, Isle of Wight

Southern Ireland

Dublin Zoo, Phoenix Park, Dublin

Fota House, Fota Island, Carrigtwohill, Cork

Glanleam Sub-tropical Gardens, Valentia Island, Co. Kerry

Mount Usher, Ashford, Co Wicklow

National Botanic Gardens, Glasnevin, Dublin

Talbot Botanic Gardens, Malahide, Dublin

Northern France

Jardin Botanique, Chateau de Vauville, Normandy

Jardin Exotique, Roscoff, Brittany

Jardin Georges Delaselle, Ile de Batz, Roscoff, Brittany

Gardens with a Mediterranean Climate

Alhambra and Generalife Gardens, Granada, Spain

Hanbury Garden, La Mortola, Ventimiglia, Northern Italy

Jardin Exotica (Cactus Garden), Monte Carlo

Jardin Exotique du Val Rahmen, Menton, Southern France

La Bambouseraie Prafrance, 30140 Generargues, Anduze, Southern France

Villa de Rothschild, Cap Ferrat, Southern France

Villa Tarranto, Lake Maggiore, Northern Italy

Isola Bella, Stressa, Lake Maggiore, Northern Italy

Isola Madre, Stressa, Lake Maggiore, Northern Italy

USA

Fairchild Tropical Gardens, Old Cutler Road, Coral Gables, Miami, Florida

Huntington Botanical Gardens, 1151 Oxford Road, San Marino, California

Longwood Gardens, Route 1, Kennett Square, Pennsylvania

Leu Botanical Gardens, Orlando, Florida

Quail Botanical Gardens, Quail Gardens Drive, Encintas, California

San Diego Zoo, San Diego, California

Suppliers of exotic-style plants

The following are UK-based nurseries that specialize in architectural and exotic-looking plants:

Abbotsbury Sub-tropical Gardens, Weymouth, Dorset DT3 4LA Tel: 01305 871344 (WS, B, F, Suc, Ban, P, Online) www.abbotsbury-tourism

Amulree Exotics, Katonia Avenue, Maylandsea, Essex CM3 6AD Tel: 01245 425255 (WS) www.turn-it-tropical.co.uk

Architectural Plants, Nuthurst, Horsham, W.Sussex, RH13 6LH Tel: 01243 545008 (WS, P, F, B, Suc, Ban) www.architecturalplants.com

Ausfern Nurseries UK Ltd, Tutherleigh House, Hubert Road, Brentwood, Essex CM14 4RF Tel: 012777 227606 (F, WS)

Brooklands Plants, 25 Treves Road, Dorchester, Dorset DT1 2HE Tel: 01305 265846 (P-seedlings)

Burncoose Nurseries, Gwennap, Redruth, Cornwall TR16 6BJ Tel: 01209 860316 (WS, Online) www.burncoose.co.uk

Devon and Dorset Bamboos, Teign Valley Nursery, Bridford, Devon Tel: 01647 252654 (B)

Drysdale Garden Exotics, Bowerwood Road, Fordingbridge, Hampshire SP6 1BN Tel: 01425 653010 (B)

Europlants UK Ltd, Great North Road, Bell Bar, Hatfield, Herts AL9 6DA Tel: 01707 649996 (WS)

Hardy Exotics Nursery, Gilly Lane, Whitecross, Penzance, Cornwall TR20 8BZ Tel: 01736 740660 (WS, P, F, Ban, Suc) www.hardyexotics.co.uk

Hart Canna, 25-27 Guildford Road West, Farnborough, Hants GU14 6PS Tel: 01252 514421 (TuP, Online) www.hartcanna.com

Jungle Giants, Burford House Gardens, Tenbury Wells, Worcestershire WR15 8HQ Tel: 01584 819885 (B)

KobaKoba, 3 Bath Road, Ashcott, Somerset TA7 9QT Tel: 01458 210700 (Ban, TuP) www.kobakoba.co.uk

Mulu Nurseries, Longdon Hill, Wickhamford, Evesham, Worcestershire WR11 7RP Tel: 01386 833171 (WS, B, TuP, Ban, Online) www.mulu.co.uk

PW Plants, Sunnyside, Heath Road, Kenninghall, Norfolk NR16 2DS Tel: 01953 888212 (WS, B)

Rosedown Mill (Plants and Exotics), Hartland, Bideford, Devon EX39 6AH Tel: 01237 441527 (P, TuP, Online) www.palmsbypost.com

Stams, The Garden House, Cappoquin, Co. Waterford, Ireland Tel: +353 5854787 (B)

The Canna Company, 14 Park Close, Mapperley, Nottingham NG3 5FB (TuP) www.cookcannas.co.uk

The Palm Centre, Ham Nursery, Ham, Richmond, Surrey, TW10 7HA Tel: 020 8255 6191 (P, WS, B, Suc, Ban, F, Online) www.palmcentre.co.uk

Trevena Cross Nurseries, Breage, Helston, Cornwall TR13 9PS Tel: 01736 763880 (WS, Suc, P, Online) www.trevenacross.co.uk

Urban Jungle, The Nurseries, Ringland Lane, Old Costessey, Norwich, Norfolk NR8 5BG Tel: 01603 744997 (WS)

Woodshoot Nurseries, Kings Bromley, Burton-upon-Trent, Staffordshire DE13 7HN Tel: 01543 472233 (WS, Suc)

KEY

B – bamboos
Ban – bananas
TuP – tuberous perennials
F – ferns
WS – wide selection
Suc – succulents
P – palms
Online – plant sales via the internet

About the author

Stephen Griffith is a trained horticulturist and landscaper, and has worked and travelled extensively in Europe, the Middle East (where he gained extensive knowledge and experience in growing exotic plants) and the UK.
Since 1990 he has been the Curator at the Abbotsbury Sub-tropical Gardens in Dorset, on England's south coast.

The garden has its own microclimate, enjoying mild, Mediterranean-like winters and long summers, enabling it to grow tender and exotic species rarely seen elsewhere in the British Isles. The 8ha (20 acre) garden retains an original 18th-century walled garden, which is surrounded by woodland, ponds and streams, dominated by vast trees and Chusan palms. There is also a Mediterranean garden and a Himalayan glade.

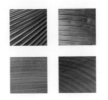

Index

TITLES AVAILABLE FROM

GMC Publications

GARDENING BOOKS

Alpine Gardening	*Chris & Valerie Wheeler*
Auriculas for Everyone: How to Grow and Show Perfect Plants	*Mary Robinson*
Beginners' Guide to Herb Gardening	*Yvonne Cuthbertson*
Beginners' Guide to Water Gardening	*Graham Clarke*
The Birdwatcher's Garden	*Hazel & Pamela Johnson*
Companions to Clematis: Growing Clematis with Other Plants	*Marigold Badcock*
Creating Contrast with Dark Plants	*Freya Martin*
Creating Small Habitats for Wildlife in your Garden	*Josie Briggs*
Exotics are Easy	*GMC Publications*
Gardening with Hebes	*Chris & Valerie Wheeler*
Gardening with Wild Plants	*Julian Slatcher*
Growing Cacti and Other Succulents in the Conservatory and Indoors	*Shirley-Anne Bell*
Growing Cacti and Other Succulents in the Garden	*Shirley-Anne Bell*
Growing Successful Orchids in the Greenhouse and Conservatory	*Mark Isaac-Williams*
Hardy Palms and Palm-Like Plants	*Martyn Graham*
Hardy Perennials: A Beginner's Guide	*Eric Sawford*
Hedges: Creating Screens and Edges	*Averil Bedrich*
Marginal Plants	*Bernard Sleeman*
Orchids are Easy: A Beginner's Guide to their Care and Cultivation	*Tom Gilland*
Plant Alert: A Garden Guide for Parents	*Catherine Collins*
Planting Plans for Your Garden	*Jenny Shukman*
Sink and Container Gardening Using Dwarf Hardy Plants	*Chris & Valerie Wheeler*
The Successful Conservatory and Growing Exotic Plants	*Joan Phelan*
Tropical Garden Style with Hardy Plants	*Alan Hemsley*
Water Garden Projects: From Groundwork to Planting	*Roger Sweetinburgh*

MAGAZINES

WOODTURNING ◆ WOODCARVING ◆ FURNITURE & CABINETMAKING
THE ROUTER ◆ NEW WOODWORKING ◆ THE DOLLS' HOUSE MAGAZINE
OUTDOOR PHOTOGRAPHY ◆ BLACK & WHITE PHOTOGRAPHY
TRAVEL PHOTOGRAPHY ◆ MACHINE KNITTING NEWS
GUILD OF MASTER CRAFTSMEN NEWS

The above represents only a selection of titles currently published or scheduled to be published.
All are available direct from the Publishers or through bookshops, newsagents and specialist retailers.
To place an order, or to obtain a complete catalogue, contact:

GMC Publications,
Castle Place, 166 High Street, Lewes, East Sussex BN7 1XU United Kingdom
Tel: 01273 488005 Fax: 01273 402866
E-mail: pubs@thegmcgroup.com

Orders by credit card are accepted